GAMES and AC for SCOUTS

ALEC. J. SPALDING
Scout Leader 'A' Troop
24th Glasgow (Bearsden) Group

First Edition – 1985
Reprinted – 1988
Reprinted – 1994

ISBN 0 85174 502 4

Printed and Made in Great Britain

CONTENTS

CHAPTER I

ABOUT THIS BOOK

The primary objective of this book is to make available a stock of interesting, exciting and thoroughly workable games and activities sufficient to provide attractive programme material for a Scout Troop for several years.

There is generally no shortage of ideas for activities for Scout programmes. Leaders will themselves get many ideas of their own from time to time while Scout literature supplies ideas in great number. It is a relatively easy matter to produce lists of ideas.

An idea is however of little value if there is not with it the means for satisfactory implementation. We may be urged to give Scouts materials in bags to identify or to try charcoal cooking but what we need to know is how to put over these suggestions as activities at a Troop meeting.

The thinking throughout this book is that no idea is a good idea if the follow through has not been done to produce a practical fully workable activity. It is because this follow through work is so often not done that many otherwise excellent ideas never appear in a Troop programme. It is our hope that in studying this book Troop Scouters will find the games and activities attractive and worthwhile but more importantly will wish to include them in programmes for the reason that the means of putting them over is spelt out in full detail.

It is of common remark that many Scout games books contain quite a number of items which are unattractive to boys and which indeed would never be offered by Scouters at a Troop meeting. This sometimes arises from over-brief or inadequate description or from the fact that an activity has not been carried forward beyond a basic idea and it has been an object of this book to translate some of these ideas into practical activities. Nevertheless we have not been looking for numbers and we have declined absolutely to repeat from any other source any game or activity which boys of Scout age are likely to regard as being juvenile or without adequate objective. Also omitted are activities which we consider to be undesirably or pointlessly violent.

Descriptions of games and activities have been written to cater for Troops of up to about 36 Scouts in six Patrols but the means of providing for lesser numbers is also covered or will be readily apparent. In general, organisation will be easier in Troops of two or three Patrols but we might be bold to suggest that the quality of meetings in such small Troops should be so good that providing a recruitment source is available, a size will soon be reached where the application of methods for full Troop numbers will be necessary.

It is not an intention to supply technical information, such as how to tie a particular knot or to read a grid reference, when this information is readily available from a convenient source. Much of the technical information required is contained in the books accompanying the Scout training programme and, in addition, technical information is available from specialist Scoutcraft books and from books on such subjects as mapping, knotting, first aid, camping, cooking and mountaineering, commonly on sale in Scout shops.

On the other hand a suitable recipe for ice-cream making is provided and exact quantities of materials used in casualty simulation are given. A purpose is to reduce to a minimum the time which people have to spend on preparation and for example a list of suggested sounds to be taped for identification is supplied and an island description is given when this is required for a particular mapping activity.

There has been a difficulty in finding a title which will convey the contents of the book with reasonable briefness. The book is a collection of games, competitions and activities. To make a precise distinction between the three headings would have little purpose even if it can be done. Activity in a broad sense can be used to include games and competitions and it is sometimes used with this meaning to give brevity in the text.

While there may be a wish to go straight to the chapters on games and activities to obtain items for next Troop meeting it will be found useful to read Chapters II and III.

Chapter II deals with the compilation of Troop meeting pro grammes and how leaders can best contribute to the running of Troop meetings. Importantly there is a section listing basic equipment required and a consideration of the place of a Patrol competition.

Chapter III is concerned with a detailed coding and classification of all items in the book and their presentation by activity type in summary tables. It will be useful to know what is implied in the coding against each game and activity and, for example, that V stands for variation with the possibility that several different programme items could be found under a title so coded while the absence of M means no special material is required other than basic equipment.

It is thought that when compiling a programme it will usually be preferred to consult these tables in Chapter III rather than the alphabetical index at the end of the book. Indeed computer enthusiasts may feel they can achieve more attractive presentation of the material with additional classifications by type, using computer equipment available to them.

The last three chapters of the book describe games and activities for camp and Troop meetings outdoors.

CHAPTER II

TROOP MEETINGS

The large majority of items described in this book are intended to be used at Troop meetings and the purpose of this chapter is to consider how the various categories of activities can best be used to build up the programme of a weekly Troop meeting and how that meeting can best be run.

Compiling the Programme

Following the opening routines which tend to be individual to Troops the first item of a Troop meeting programme will be one in which all the Scouts take part. This has the effect of establishing a feeling of togetherness which may have been lost over the week. Most likely to fill this need is a game in which everyone is more or less continually involved such as Corner Ball, Prisoner's Base, Pass Faster or Time in Centre as chosen from Chapter IV on active games to be played by the whole Troop.

Every Troop meeting should contain at least one item as a result of which a boy can go home feeling he has learnt something new and such an activity can well come next in the programme. This might be one of the direct learning activities such as the national grid, a particular knot, or some stick tricks as described in Chapter VI though most of the construction and display items given in Chapters VII and VIII have a learning element as well as an intensive level of Patrol operation.

Unless the previous activity has been particularly energetic, when a restful game would be appropriate, the next programme item is likely best to be a short active game taken either again from Chapter IV or perhaps from Chapter XII on relay formation games.

There may then be a fairly short period, say a quarter of an hour, in Patrol corners when Patrol Leaders can assess progress being made by their Scouts in badge work and the Scouts have the opportunity to learn and pass various items. Leaders may help at this stage with classes for Scouts from various Patrols and in other ways as required. Alternatively this period might be occupied with a multi-project as in Chapter IX.

The Patrol corner period can lead on to a Patrol based answer finding competition such as Similar Pictures or more actively True or False from Chapter X. By this time people will be happy to take a rest and the active end game before closing can be one in which not everyone is continuously occupied such as Heady Handball or Floor Ball from Chapter V.
A typical Troop meeting might therefore be as follows:

7.30 p.m.	Opening routines
7.45 p.m.	Active game involving everyone at the same time
8.00 p.m.	Learning activity with follow-up competition or a construction, display or cooking activity
8.25 p.m.	Short active game
8.35 p.m.	Patrol corner period or activity such as a multi-project
8.50 p.m.	Answer finding competition
9.00 p.m.	Active game not necessarily occupying everyone simultaneously
9.20 p.m.	Closing routines

In choosing the precise game or activity for a particular stage of the programme care must be taken that all items suitably integrate with each other. One of the most important skills of programme compiling is to ensure there is an appropriate mixture and follow on between learning and recreational activities as well as between active and non-active games and activities.

The exercise of Patrol Leadership and the functioning of Scouts effectively in a Patrol might be held by many people to be the main training feature of the Scout programme and for this reason there is constant emphasis in this book on ways of using games and activities for this purpose. So important is this aspect of Scouting regarded that activities which call for particularly intense Patrol operation have been coded under the letter I. In fact to have more than one such coded activity in a Troop meeting programme could cause exhaustion in a Patrol as well as perhaps discouragement to a Patrol Leader who was not very good at it.

Some items intended for a particular programme space take longer than others. In many combinations of games and activities the example programme given above would be over-crowded and not possible of achievement. The different capability of Scouts and their approach to items is an important factor here. In some cases the situation will be met by dropping out one item such as in this case the 8.50 p.m. answer finding competition. On the other hand if the Troop is small some items will certainly not take so long. Thus if there are only two Patrols the 20 minutes allotted for the 9 p.m. active game will be in excess of requirement.

A modification to the example programme which may often be necessary is the amalgamation of the time for the 8 p.m. learning activity and the 8.35 p.m. Patrol corner activity. This combined time, or at least part of it, will be required for some cooking activities, probably for trestle making and racing and for the large scale multi-project Business Manufacture. Indeed some activities can be of a length which will absorb almost the whole of a meeting leaving time perhaps for additionally only a beginning and an end game.

Sometimes it will be found that an activity is popular and successful beyond expectation. In these circumstances there will probably be disappointment if more time is not allowed for something which is going so well. The programme is not sacrosanct and there is normally no reason why an item should not be dropped out. This will be advantageous all round. The Scouts have been satisfied with what they got while the leaders are in the happy position of being able to go home with an item still in the bag all ready to be produced at a future meeting without further effort.

There are some activities which because they require equipment which is available only in limited quantity or because detailed specialist instruction has to be given cannot be done by all members of the Troop at the same time. An example of this is mouth-to-mouth ventilation, and activities of this kind can be covered by means of a circuit type programme where the Troop is divided into three sections, perhaps of two Patrols each.

The organisation of circuit programmes is described in Chapter XIII and while they give a change from normal Troop meetings they must not be overdone. Scouts like a degree of routine in Troop meetings and do not welcome excessive departures from what they are expecting. In a more extreme example it is well known that a Troop meeting taking the form of an outing to some place of interest may, if previously announced, be poorly attended on the grounds that it is not a "proper" Troop meeting.

It will be the case that some games and activities are more popular than others and there are demands for repetition. This really amounts to no more than saying what is inevitable that some games are better than others, and there is no reason why established favourites such as perhaps Corner Ball and Heady Handball should not be played once a month or so. Integrated with these are the large number of activities which gain from their novelty and interest and which for this reason may only be included in the programme perhaps once in two years.

In order to assist in the selection of games and activities to form an attractive programme all items have been coded and classified as described in Chapter III.

Equipment

In classifying the games and activities the identifying letter M has been used to indicate those for which special material or equipment is required. Examples are cooking activities or learning roller bandaging. Activities of this kind are among the most worthwhile and it is essential that the effort is made to obtain what is needed to include them in the programme at the appropriate time. Much equipment so obtained or made up will be kept in store and there will thus be the great advantage that it will not have to be acquired or prepared whenever it is desired to repeat activities in the future.

At the other end of the scale there are games and activities which require nothing more specialist than chalk or a ball. The majority of items in this book are intermediate between the two extremes and are intended to be carried out with what might be termed basic Scout equipment. It is of great importance that this equipment be available in adequate quantity. Shortages will inevitably result in poor programmes and frustration that interesting items cannot be done.

Equipment for running interesting and worthwhile meetings will be the first priority on Troop funds. Given below is the list of equipment required including some which may have been purchased as items of equipment to be used at camp.

Indoor Footballs — Lightweight indoor footballs at the rate of at least one per Patrol but most preferably two per Patrol with a minimum of eight footballs in total. Half the footballs should be distinguishable from the other half by colour but greater distinction by colour can be advantageous for some activities.

Scout Staves — These should be available at the rate of six per Patrol or one per Scout in the Troop whichever total number is the greater. There should be at least two 5 ft. staves per Patrol.

Knotting/Lashing Ropes — These ropes must be at least 8 ft.

long, though not exceeding 10 ft. and should be available at the rate of at least nine per Patrol. Firm whipping of the ends of the ropes is essential. The ropes must not be too thick for making firm lashings on Scout staves.

Rope Lengths — Two 50 ft. lengths of rope of knotting rope thickness should be available for each Patrol.

Paper — A stock of A4 white paper should be available for general use.

Pencils — If it is not an established tradition that every Scout carries a pencil than there must be a stock sufficient to issue one to every Scout.

Chalk — A reasonable supply of white chalk is needed plus a small stock of chalk of different colours equal to the number of Patrols.

Skittles — 14 good standing skittles.

Small Plastic Balls — A stock of hollow plastic balls with holes to impede flight at the rate of one per Scout but with a minimum of 36. The balls may be of the gamester size (2½ ins. in diameter) or the teamster size (3½ ins. in diameter) or a mixture of both. It is sometimes useful to have balls of different colours.

Wood batons — About 14 round wooden batons about 1 in. thick and 14 ins. long.

Grommets — Two rope grommets about 1 in. thick and 6½ ins. outside diameter.

Tenniquoit Rings — Two tenniquoit rings about 1 in. thick and 6½ ins. outside diameter per Patrol.

Gymshoes — Old discarded gymshoes at a number roughly equal to half the membership of the Troop.

Candles — Stock of at least one dozen candles.

Wood Blocks — Blocks of wood measuring 10 ins. x 6 ins. x 4 ins. at the rate of two per Patrol.

Wool — Supply of red, green and yellow wool for use as lives or trail purposes in wide games.

Compasses — One Silva type compass per Patrol.

Maps — Ordnance survey 1:50,000 map of the same area for each Patrol. This will often most suitably be the local map.

Balloons — Good supply of round balloons and smaller supply of long balloons.

Hawser — A length of hawser may have been obtained primarily for pioneering projects at camp. It will also have a use in some Troop meeting activities.

Stoves and Cooking Utensils — There are a number of Troop meeting cooking activities which will require two stoves per Patrol and also a supply of dixies, frying pans and flips. These are likely to be available from the Troop stock of camp equipment.

Putting over the Programme

It will be found that there are frequent references in descriptions of games and activities to the function of leaders in explaining to Scouts what is to be done and in acting as judges, umpires and referees.

Many a game or activity is spoilt by inadequate explanation or by unsatisfactory judging, umpiring or refereeing. Even an apparently simple game like British Bulldogs can be badly run. It has been an intention of high priority in this book to provide the vital detail which will ensure that a programme item is a success because everyone concerned with it knows what they are supposed to do. When a programme item is chosen it is recommended that not only is the full description read under that particular heading, but also the general description at the beginning of the chapter. In some instances where items are similar it will be found that fuller detail is given for the first item of a chapter.

It may sometimes be felt that the running of an item to an ideal standard requires a level of staffing which may not always be available. There may of course be situations where people are just not available to help but it can be a common position that there is a lack of helpers for the reason that they are given virtually nothing to do or because they find that what they are asked to do is above or below their present capability. In studying this book it will be realised that in acting as judges, umpires or referees or in doing such things as correcting competitions there is in helping to run a Troop meeting an immense range of experience and ability required from in fact the quite elementary. This is advantageous as it gives new leaders the opportunity to learn by experience. The situation is a particularly favourable one for Venture Scouts or other leaders who may be assisting with the Troop and who can gain immensely from this on-the-job experience and training. It is suggested that this book will be found of particular value to new leaders for whom it is especially important that they get the detail right.

In addition to knowing what they are supposed to be doing it is of great importance also that those involved with running a Troop meeting know when they are supposed to be doing it. A gap in the programme can spoil the whole rhythm of a meeting and it is essential therefore that those concerned with the next item be on hand with the necessary equipment ready to get it going without break in continuity.

Patrol Competition

In virtually all the items described in the chapters ahead there is reference to points being awarded and there is often quite detailed consideration of how judging a particular competition should be done. It is most important that those judging competitions are quite clear on what they are giving points for and here again it is intended that the book should help on this.

Emphasis is placed on the proper awarding of points for the reason that it is assumed that there is in progress an inter-Patrol competition. Some points will probably be given for an initial inspection but most of the points will be gained from the games and competitions held during meetings. Probably a month is the best length of time between announcements of results.

Too much stress should not be placed on winning the overall Patrol competition or on individual items for the reason that only one Patrol can win and constantly coming low down the list can cause disheartenment. Rather the emphasis should be placed on everyone doing well and it should for example be pleasing to be able to report that all Patrols made good trestles for chariot racing and gained seven, eight or nine points. The actual racing may only add a maximum of a further four points and the idea that hopefully can be put over is that the whole Troop is getting better and will therefore be able to undertake more interesting activities requiring a higher state of proficiency.

CHAPTER III

CLASSIFICATION BY TYPES

All games and activities have been coded in order that there can be easy recognition of type from titles in the text and in the index. In addition the coding has been used to list items by type in summary tables later in this chapter and it is suggested that consulting these tables will be found the quickest and simplest way of selecting an activity for any particular part of a programme.

Given below is the key to letters used in coding. As far as possible the first letter of the preferred descriptive word has been used. Where in order to achieve differentiation the first letter of a preferred word cannot be used then the similar word from which the letter is taken is given in brackets.

A — Active	M — Special Material
N — Non-Active	E — Long (extended)
L — Learning	S — Short
I — Intensive Patrol	K — Cooking
R — Recreational	Y — Relay Formation
C — Competition	O — Camp and Troop Meetings Outdoors
P — Part of Troop	
T — Circuit (travel)	V — Variation

All activities are first classified as either Active (A) or Non-Active (N).

The descriptions L for Learning and I for Intensive Patrol are applied to Active and Non-Active games and activities.

R for Reacreational is used only with active games and is intended to make distinction from L where knowledge or a skill of some kind has to be acquired or displayed.

Similarly C for Competition is used only for non-active items in making distinction from L.

M means that material other than basic equipment listed in Chapter II is required. Sometimes this may not present a particular difficulty with perhaps only copies of a newspaper or packs of cards to be obtained.

E for Long (extended) means that the activity is likely to take more than about 45 minutes. The description has not however been used in respect of outdoor activities where the time taken can often be very much a matter of choice.

S items are intended to last not more than about five minutes. They may be used as emergency fillers. Some other items can be made short merely by playing them for not very long but in some cases this can be dis-satisfying.

V for Variation against an item can be important in indicating that there may be several additional activities under one heading.

All games and activities in the book have been included once only, in one or other of the summary tables headed as follows.

Active Recreational	AR
Active Intensive Patrol	AI
Active Learning	AL
Non-Active Learning	NL
Non-Active Intensive Patrol	NI
Non-Active Competition	NC
Camp and Troop Meetings Outdoors	O

The titles of the first six tables supply the first two letters of the coding of items in these titles. All outdoor games and activities have been grouped together in a final table on the grounds that the fact that an activity is outdoors will usually be the determining consideration in its choice.

Descriptions of activities are found by looking up the number given to the left of titles listed in the tables.

Active Recreational

No.	Title	Code
1.	Corner Ball	AR
2.	Progressive Push	AR
3.	Quarters	ARV
4.	Bucket Cricket	AR
5.	Box Cricket	AR
6.	Poisonous Ground	AR
7.	Prisoner's Base	AR
8.	British Bulldogs	AR
9.	Pass Faster	AR
10.	Time in Centre	ARV
11.	Tail Tag	AR
12.	Skittles in Centre	AR
13.	Box Ball	AR
14.	Port and Starboard	AR
15.	One, Two and Three	AR
16.	Off the Floor	AR
17.	Crosses in Circle	ARS
25.	King Ball	AR
26.	Baton Ball	AR
27.	Sack Tug	AR
28.	Three Against One	ARS
29.	Torpedoeing	AR
30.	Time Hike	ARS
31.	Line Toss	AR
32.	Skittle Ball	ARP
33.	Floor Ball	ARP
34.	Drive Ball	ARP
35.	Logger	ARP
36.	Heady Handball	ARP
37.	Push Grommet	ARP
38.	Volley Ball	ARP
39.	Curtain Ball	ARP
40.	Bench Pursuit	ARP
123.	Bench Relay	ARY

No.	Activity	Code
18.	Gladiators	ARS
19.	Rope Whirl Jump	AR
20.	Shoulder Push	AR
21.	Contra Activities	ARS
22.	Three Corner Grab	AR
23.	Three Corner Tug	AR
24.	Three Way Hawser Tug	AR
124.	Staggers Relay	ARY
125.	Stepping Stone Relay	ARY
127.	Numbers Relay	ARMY
129.	Highland Games	ARMY
130.	Progressive Leap	ARY
151.	Stave Bowls	ART

Active Intensive Patrol

No.	Activity	Code
64.	Trestle Making and Racing	AIL
65.	Height from Ground	AI
66.	Wigan Flagstaff	AIL
67.	Stave Bundling	AIL
68.	Balloon Bombing	AI
69.	Candle Lighting	AI
70.	Object Retrieval	AIM
74.	Stretcher Making Activities	AILV
75.	Gymnastic Display	AIL
76.	Drill Display	AIL
77.	Marching Display	AILM
78.	Skipping Display	AI
79.	Scout Staff Display	AI
80.	Moving Injured Persons Display	AIL
82.	Letters and Numbers	AI
162.	Incident in Circuit	AIMV

Active Learning

No.	Activity	Code
44.	Moving Injured Persons	AL
51.	Rope Crawl	AL
52.	Stick Tricks	ALV
53.	Stave Exchange	AL
57.	Rescue Line	AL
71.	Pharaoh's Chariot	AL
72.	Stilts with Staves	AL
73.	Stilts with Tins	ALM
111.	True or False	ALV
112.	Animal, Vegetable or Mineral	ALV
113.	Object Bringing	ALV
126.	Tenniquoit Relay	ALY
128.	Hammer & Nails Relay	ALMY
131.	Stretcher Relay	ALY
132.	Four Handed Seat Relay	ALY
133.	Pharaoh's Chariot Relay	ALY
134.	Tree Identification Relay	ALMYV
135.	Rescue Line Relay	ALY
136.	Stilts Relay	ALMY
137.	Street Knowledge Relay	ALMY
142.	Rope Stretcher	ALT
143.	Line Coiling and Throwing	ALT
145.	Belay System	ALTM
146.	Abseiling	ALTM
159.	Moving Injured Persons (Circuit)	ALTV
163.	Volley Ball (Circuit)	ALT

Non-Active Learning

No.	Activity	Code
41.	National Grid	NL
42.	Knot Learning	NLV
43.	Morse Code	NLMV
45.	Tree Identification	NLMV
46.	Badge Scheme Progress	NL
47.	Sling Tying	NL
48.	Local Knowledge	NLM
49.	Parcelling	NLM
50.	Paper Cup	NLM
141.	Holger-Neilsen Resuscitation	NLT
147.	Paraffin Pressure Stoves and Lamps	NLTM
148.	Knots and Lashings (Circuit)	NLT
149.	Splicing	NLT
152.	Estimating Inaccessible Widths and Heights	NLT

54. Dimensions Estimating NLMV
55. Weights Estimating NLM
56. Numbers Estimating NLM
58. Casualty Simulation NLMEV
59. Square and Diagonal Lashings NL
60. Figure-of-Eight Lashing NL
61. Rolling Hitch NL
62. Splicing NL
63. Circuit Learning NL
138. Roller Bandaging NLTM
139. Mouth-to-Mouth Resuscitation NLTM
140. Recovery Position NLT
157. Cane Pioneering NLTM
158. Guide Badge (Circuit) NLTM
160. Cooking Activities (Circuit) NLTMKV
161 Badge Scheme Progress (Circuit) NLTV
165. Shrove Tuesday Pancakes NLMK
166. Mixed Grill (Cooking) NLMKV
167. Chinese Cooking NLMKV
168. Dessert Cooking NLMKV
169. Baking NLMKV
170. Cooking with Almonds NLMK
171. Cooking with Candles NLMK
177. Ice-cream making NLMEK

Non-Active Intensive Patrol

81. Tableaux NILV
83. Object Construction NIM
84. Pipe Cleaner Objects NIM
85. Making the Greatest NIM
86. Business Manufacture NIME

Non-Active Competition

87. Shoe Identification NC
88. Photograph Identification NCMV
89. Point Identification NC
90. Kim's Game NC
91. Pelmanism NCM
92. Premises in Street NCM
93. Kim's Game Shapes NC
94. Island Description NCV
95. Knot Advance NCV
96. Similar Pictures NCM
97. Leader Description NCS
98. Round the Hall Naming NCS
99. Prince of Wales Slipper NC
100. Puzzles and Quizzes NCMV
101. Slide Identifications NCMV
102. Noughts and Crosses NCV
103. Periwinkle NCV
104. Finger-Print Identification NCM
105. Footprint Identification NC
106. Potato Prints NCM
107 Sound Identifications NCM
108. Sandpaper Coarseness NCM
109. Newspaper Information NCM
110. Newspaper Words NCM
114. Passing Round Activities NCM
115. Contents of Bags NCM
116. Picture Cards NCMV
117. Dimensions Passing Round NCM
118. Weights Passing Round NCM
119. Numbers Passing Round NCM
120. Tree Twigs Passing Round NCMV
121. Paint Colours NCM
122. Object Passing Round NCM
144. Kim's Game Change NCT
150. Stave Extrication NCT
153. Balls into Circle NCT
154. Clove Hitch in Circle NCT
155. Rolling Hitch in Circle NCT
156. Advertisement Making NCTM
164. Sound Identifications (Circuit) NCTM

Camp and Troop Meeting Outdoors

172. Cooking without Utensils NLMKOV
173. Cooking with Aluminium Foil NLMKOV
174. Cooking with Charcoal NLMKOV
175. Rabbit Skinning and Cooking NLMKO
176. Pigeon Cooking NLMKO
178. Release ARO
179. Besieged Stockade AROV
180. Wall Sabotage ARO
181. Strategic Crossing AI
182. Territory Crossing ARO
183. Water Carrying ARMO
184. Vehicle Ambush ARMO
185. Lion and Hunters ARO
186. Prince Charlie ARO
187. Camp Cricket ARO
188. Camp Golf ARMO
189. Tenniquoit ARMO
190. Relay Message ALO
191. Kim's Game Matching AIO
192. Holes in the Road ALO
193. Tree Registration AIO
194. Gaining Ground ARO
195. Athlete Badge ALO
196. Naval Battle NCMO
197. Competitions in Tents NCMOV
198. Night Sabotage AROV
199. Night Attack AROV
200. Night Hike Interception AROV
201. Morse Code Night Games ALOV
202. Incident Journey AIMOV

CHAPTER IV

ACTIVE GAMES FOR WHOLE-TROOP

It is important that all Scouts should have the feeling that they are taking part in a Troop meeting right from the start and for this reason a game at the beginning of a meeting should normally be one in which everyone is involved continuously or at least one in which there is prospect of play or of resumed play for everyone at any moment. This is in distinction from games where there may be two sides playing with six Scouts in each and there is inevitably waiting for a turn to play.

Active games involving the whole Troop are also useful after a sedentary inter-Patrol competition or to give a feeling of togetherness again after Scouts have been dispersed on different activities.

1. Corner Ball **AR**

Goals are set up in each Patrol corner consisting of a bench about 8 ft. long turned on its side and laid across the corner with the top outwards. If there are six Patrols goals can be set up mid-way along each side of the hall by placing one end of a bench against the wall and angling the bench out at 45°. No doubt a row of chairs could also be used to form goals.

Patrols stand behind their benches and the Scouts are carefully numbered so that as far as possible Scouts of similar size in different Patrols have the same number. Also if, for example, the largest Patrol has seven Scouts then some Scouts in smaller Patrols are given two numbers to bring them up to seven. The extra numbers are likely to be given to small Scouts so that they match the small boys at the end of the large Patrol.

A football is placed in the centre of the hall and a number called. The Scouts of that number, playing football amongst themselves, endeavour to kick the ball against the face of the bench of their opponents while at the same time preventing their own bench being hit. If a ball goes over a bench and in among the non-playing members of a Patrol the ball must be immediately punched out into the middle of the hall.

This can be a very popular game which may be especially liked by those younger Scouts who enjoy playing good standard football. Some numbers should be re-called to keep everyone on the alert.

Two points should be awarded to the winner and one point to the runner-up each time and the score accumulated.

2. Progressive Push **AR**

The Troop room is divided into eight equal sized rectangles by means of a line down the centre and by three lines across the hall marking quarter lengths. The rectangles are labelled from one end 8, 7, 6, 5 down one side and then across to 4 at the other end and continuing 3, 2, 1 down the other side so that 1 is adjacent to 8.

All members of the Troop gather in rectangle 8 and on the call to start endeavour to push other members into the next lower number rectangle while themselves remaining in the high number rectangle.

Initially the game may be rather vigorous as large and small Scouts are together in rectangle 8. However, the tendency is for smaller Scouts to be pushed fairly rapidly into the lower number rectangles where they contest among themselves while the larger Scouts remain contesting in the first few higher number rectangles.

The slightest touch by any part of the person over the line means moving to the next square. No one may hold on to any part of the building or its furnishings. About four minutes will probably be a long enough period of play including a warning of approaching expiry of time. This is in fact a good inter-Patrol game with Patrols assisting their own Scouts and combining to push members of other Patrols into next rectangles.

The method of scoring at the end is important. On the sounding of the final whistle everyone remains stationary in the rectangles in which they are. The members of each Patrol raise their hands in turn and a total score is obtained by adding the number for each Scout according to the rectangle in which he is in. This is then divided by the numbers of persons in the Patrol to give an average to one decimal place. 4, 3, 2 and 1 points are then awarded to Patrols in descending order of highest average with, for example, 2½ points to two Patrols if they are tying in second place.

3. Quarters **ARV**

As conceived to be played by four Patrols the hall is divided into quarters by lines drawn centrally down the length and across the width.

A lightweight football is thrown up in the hall and it is the objective for each Patrol to expel the ball as quickly as possible from their own quarter. After an interval of between five and 20 seconds a whistle is blown by a leader who is facing away from play. The Patrol in whose quarter the ball is when the whistle is blown is awarded one negative point by a leader who is closely observing the play. The game continues in a similar manner with points being carefully recorded against each Patrol until one accumulates five negative points. The Patrol with least negative points at that state is the winner. Two or three sessions may be played.

An interesting variation which gives more intensive participation especially if numbers are over 20 is to play with two footballs which must be distinguishable by colour. While only one person continues to blow the whistle it is necessary to have an additional referee so that each ball can be followed separately.

There is in fact no reason why the game should only be played by four Patrols and the hall can be divided up into areas for any number of Patrols from two upwards. There is a disadvantage in having an area in the centre of the hall as against at the end and if for example six Patrols are playing then there should be three sessions with Patrols moving round one place clockwise each time.

4. Bucket Cricket **AR**

Although the original name suggests the use of an upturned bucket the game is more satisfactorily played using a round or square metal drum standing about 14 ins. high and 9 ins. across. The bat consists of a piece of wood about 20 ins. long and 2½ ins. wide and the game is played with a tennis ball or a rubber ball of similar size. A circle is drawn ideally about 25 ft. in diameter and the drum placed in the centre.

Patrols distribute round the edge of the circle but with the Patrol members intermixed. The first Patrol to bat leaves the circle and the first batsman stands on the drum. Bowling must always be underhand and must be from outside the circle. The batsman must be given the opportunity to face his first bowl but not to face bowls thereafter. For every bowl made the batsman gains one run unless he is out with that bowl. If the batsman strikes the ball he gains a further one run. It is permissible for a bowler to make to bowl but not to release the ball. Such action is, however, considered a bowl and counts as one run. Also the ball may be deliberately passed across the circle but this again counts as one run. A batsman is out bowled by the ball hitting the drum, caught, played on or by falling off the drum.

The bowler is the player to whom the ball comes naturally after the previous bowl. If the bowl should not reach the edge of the circle an umpire instructs a nearby player to retrieve the ball for the next bowl. No balls, counting as an additional run, are called for bowls delivered with any part of the bowler's person touching the floor within the circle or for throwing or not bowling underhand. A batsman cannot be out with a no ball.

When all members of the first Patrol have batted the Patrol returns to their positions in the circle and their total chalked up. The next Patrol then leaves the circle. It can give added interest to determine the order of batting by a member of the duty Patrol being called forward to take a name out of a hat. Uneven numbers in Patrols can be made up by allowing some Scouts to bat twice. If there are six or more Patrols and there is enough space it is a good idea to have separate games at each end of the hall in order to maximise participation.

5 Box Cricket **AR**

This is played in a similar manner to Bucket Cricket except that the batsman stands on a strong box varying from about 24 ins. square to roughly 30 ins. by 18 ins. and 18 ins. high. In this case the bat is an ordinary cricket bat and the ball is an indoor lightweight football. As in Bucket Cricket there is restriction to underarm bowling. This is a good game. It may be preferred to Bucket Cricket as being rather more robust and it is well worthwhile to obtain a suitable box to be available for this game.

6. Poisonous Ground **AR**

This game is not an inter-Patrol game and has the disadvantage that some Scouts are out from an early stage. It does however have an attraction for some Scouts and merits occasional playing.

The game is best played in duplicate with the bigger Scouts linking hands to form a circle at one end of the hall and the smaller Scouts a circle at the other end. In the centre of each circle there is designated an area of poisonous ground. This might take the form of two crossed mattresses each measuring 6 ft. by 2 ft. There may also be one or two poisonous weeds between the arms of the crossed mattresses represented by a stick with a hat on top standing in a large bottle.

The object of the game is to make other players touch the poisonous articles while avoiding doing so oneself. A player is out if he makes the slightest touch on any of the poisonous materials. There can be a tendency to part hands in the game and it is a desirable rule that if the same two hands part twice then both players involved are out. The poisonous area can be reduced in size as the circle gets smaller.

7. Prisoner's Base **AR**

This is a well known game and is a good one because of the continuous participation which it allows for everyone.

The Troop room is divided into four equal sections by three lines drawn across the length. For description these are named A, B, C and D from one end to the other.

Half the Patrols of the Troop go into section B and half into section C as far as possible giving equal total numbers. A lightweight football is thrown into section B or C (but B is assumed) and a player in B throws the ball to hit any player in section C. A player in section C is out if he is hit, without the ball having touched the floor, on any part of his person except his hands, by an opponent's throw. A player who is out in section C continues to play however by immediately going to section A and throwing the ball from there to hit those in section B who are now under attack from two sides. Similarly those in section B as they are got out by throws from sections A or C go to section D.

No player may leave his section to get a ball except that a player from B may go into A and a player from C into D if, as may happen at an early stage in a game, there are no players in A or D sections.

No player may move holding the ball. After the ball has been caught or picked up one pass may be made to another player within the section. The ball may be passed across sections B or C to D or A if this is thought advantageous.

One point should be given to the Patrols of the winning side. Two sessions of the game may be welcome. Although sounding a little complicated in description the method of play fairly readily becomes apparent.

8. British Bulldogs **AR**

This is a vigorous well known game which does sometimes have a place in Troop programmes.

Chalk lines are marked across the hall about 10 ft. from each end although a lesser distance will suffice if the hall is short.

The Troop goes behind one of the lines and a single heavily built Scout or better, we think a complete Patrol if the Troop is large, stands in the centre area. It can be appropriate for the duty Patrol for the evening to do this.

On the blowing of a start whistle the Scouts behind the line endeavour to get across the centre space and behind the line at the other end without being caught by the Scouts in the middle. Being caught consists of being lifted clear of the floor long enough for the words British Bulldogs to be called. Scouts caught join those in the centre and assist in the catching of the remaining Scouts as they make succeeding runs until all are caught, the last caught being the winner.

A Scout making the slightest touch over an end line is considered to be across. A further rule is that everyone makes his way across entirely independently. Catching proceeds irrespective of the Patrol a Scout is in and it is not appropriate to award points as part of an inter-Patrol competition.

It is important to allow time for all Scouts held in the centre to be lifted clear of the floor and for the Scouts in the centre to have taken up ready positions before the whistle is sounded for a return run. Even so it may sometimes be that some particularly large Scouts are virtually uncatchable. Announcement may be made that the game will be concluded after another two runs.

9. Pass Faster **AR**

Two Patrols with their members alternating stand round the edge of a large circle. A different coloured football is provided for each Patrol and given to Scouts on opposite sides of the circle. On instruction to start the Scouts holding balls pass them to the next Scout in their Patrol clockwise round the circle. The passing continues with the objective of overtaking the ball of the other Patrol. A faultily passed ball or a dropped ball must be recovered by the Scout who was receiving it and he then passes it onwards from his correct stance. When one ball passes the other a point is awarded and the game restarted from opposite sides of the circle. The winner is the one with most points at the end of the playing period.

If there are six Patrols the game should be played in triplicate if there is enough room and a total of six footballs will be required of different colour in each of the three sets of two. Exactly equal numbers must play each other and Patrols being of the same numbers should as far as possible be paired off together. If one is left with say a Patrol of six against a Patrol of five then five play against five and one member of the six Patrol sits out in rotation at each re-start. The game is rather inconvenient for a Troop with an uneven number of Patrols. It should be noted that if two Patrols with even numbers of players are playing each other it is not possible to place the balls exactly opposite in the circle and care should be taken that the one place advantage is alternated between the Patrols at re-start.

10. Time in Centre **ARV**

This game and the three games which follow are all to be classified as active and have the similarity that they are played in a circle with each Patrol in turn endeavouring to achieve the best timed performance.

Where there are six or more Patrols, and if space allows, the game should be played in duplicate in order to maximise participation.

The Troop stands round the outside of a circle about 25 ft. in diameter with members of Patrols intermixed. Each Patrol in turn goes into the circle and the objective is to remain for as long as possible without being hit by a lightweight football thrown by the other players from outside the circle.

Players in the centre may protect themselves by punching away the ball but it may not be caught or thrown. A player in the centre leaves the circle immediately he is hit on any part of his person other than the hands. In practice the ball will rarely move slowly or come to rest within the circle but it is in any case a rule that the players within the circle must immediately punch the ball out of the circle.

Careful timing is made for each Patrol from the time the first ball is thrown at them until the last person is out. A time limit is not usually required but if need be one can be set at two minutes and if more than one Patrol survives to the time limit then the winner is the one which has had the smallest percentage of their number knocked out. Slightly different numbers in Patrols does not matter seriously as the greater degree of congestion in the circle generally causes the first members of a large Patrol to be got out quickly.

A variation of this game is that players in the centre are not allowed to touch the ball even with their hands. A ball becoming slow or dead in the circle can be retrieved by a player standing round the outside of the circle.

11. Tail Tag **AR**

The Troop takes up position as for Time in Centre. In this case when the Patrol goes in the centre the second member of the Patrol grips the Patrol Leader with both arms round his waist. The succeeding Scouts grip similarly the person in front to form a low lying tail behind the Patrol Leader who remains erect. The players outside the circle in this game have to hit with the indoor football any part of the person of the player at the end of the tail. Immediately the end person is hit he leaves the circle. The next end person has then to be hit and so on until only the Patrol Leader is left who is finally eliminated as in the individual free running Time in Centre game.

The time of survival of each Patrol is carefully noted. There may be a rather greater need to use a time limit in Tail Tag than in Time in Centre. The skill of the game is for the Patrol Leader always to turn to face the ball and the tail to wheel so that they are protected by the Patrol Leader who may punch the ball away.

12. Skittles in Centre **AR**

Again a circle ideally about 25 ft. in diameter is used and the Troop stands round the outside as in the two previous games. A circle 8 ft. in diameter is drawn in the centre of the large circle and four skittles are stood inside the small circle equally spaced about 2 ft. 6 ins. from the circumference. No player may enter the small circle.

The first Patrol to be timed enters the ring between the two circles and their aim is to prevent for as long as possible the other players from knocking over the skittles with a football thrown from outside the large circle. The defending Patrol can intercept the ball in any way they wish. They must immediately expel the ball to outside the large circle by any means except kicking. In the rare circumstance of the ball being marooned in the small circle then it is retrieved and expelled by the defenders to outside the large circle on the instructions of the umpire. A skittle is counted down if this is the result of the play of a defender.

The winner is the Patrol which can keep at least one of its skittles standing for the longest time or has the most standing at the end of a time limit. An advantage of this game is that no one is out at any stage.

13. Box Ball **AR**

This can be the most popular in this series of games. Like Skittles in Centre it has the advantage that nobody is out for any part of the time.

Very suitable equipment is four tea chests. These are placed touching each other with the open end upwards in a square in the centre of a circle about 9 ft. in diameter. As for the other games the Patrols stand inter-mixed around an outer circle ideally about 25 ft. in diameter.

Each Patrol takes it in turn to go into the ring formed by the two circles. No player may enter the smaller circle. About six footballs are spread round the Patrols on the outer circle and the objective is for these Patrols to throw all the footballs into one or other of the tea chests. Some accuracy in throwing is required and the defending Patrol intercepts balls as best it can. Balls are expelled to the outside of the large circle, or taken from the small circle, as described for Skittles in Centre. The winning Patrol is the one which keeps out at least one football for the longest time or if a time limit is applied has most footballs still in play at the end of the time limit.

No doubt other receptacles than tea chests can be used but it is important that they present a throw of suitable difficulty and that balls do not bounce out. It is unlikely the equipment will be available to play this game in duplicate and the two sets of footballs would have to be distinguishable.

14. Port and Starboard **AR**

Lines are drawn across the hall about 6 ft. from each end. One of the boxes so formed is designated port and the other starboard.

On the call "port" all Scouts of the Troop run to enter the port box and on the call "starboard" they go to the starboard box. In addition if the call "man overboard" is made everyone as quickly as possible lies flat on the floor wherever they are.

A leader makes the calls successively in any order he chooses and with varying lengths of time between so that sometimes no one can complete the instruction before turning to another and sometimes virtually everyone completes it. Every few calls, or occasionally sometimes even after only one call, the leader decides that a call has been the last of a series and the last Scout to complete that instruction is out. The game proceeds until only one is left.

If numbers are large or if it is desired to keep the game short two Scouts may be put out each time in the early stages. Also, especially in the latter stages, it can avoid any feeling of invidiousness and add to spectator interest if one leader, making the calls, keeps his face to a wall while another leader indicates who is out.

Inter-Patrol points can be awarded for the last few Scouts in.

15. One, Two and Three **AR**

Lines are drawn across the four corners of the hall forming triangles large enough for all the Troop to get into fairly easily and the game is started by the Troop going to one corner.

In whatever corner the Troop may be at a particular time they proceed to the corner across the hall on the call "one", to the corner down the length of the hall on the call "two" and to the corner diagonally opposite on the call of "three".

Varying intervals are made between calls and the game proceeds as described for Port and Starboard.

16. Off the Floor **AR**

For this game the Troop is told that on the calling of a Patrol name and the instruction "off the floor" the other Patrols of the Troop have 30 seconds to remove all members of the called Patrol from contact with the floor. Any member of the called Patrol who has any part of his person in contact with the floor when the whistle is blown after 30 seconds gains one point.

It is sometimes suggested that the game can extend over the whole Troop meeting period but such an arrangement is likely to be undesirably disruptive and to spoil other good activities. The game is best used to provide interludes in some other specific game or activity.

The game can for example be played during the course of Port and Starboard and One, Two and Three where it has the advantage of involving those who have been put out of these games. It can also, again for example, be used to provide interludes in a session of formal drill instruction should such an activity ever be required.

It is important to make it clear beforehand that after the score for each Patrol has been counted everyone takes up exactly the position they were in before the call. No one may leave the Troop room.

17. Crosses in Circles **ARS**

A circle 3 ft. in diameter is drawn in each Patrol corner with chalk of different colour and the chalk given to the Patrol Leader. The Patrol Leader divides the chalk among his Patrol as desired and the object of the game is to make crosses in the circle of opposing Patrols while at the same time preventing crosses being made in the Patrol's own circle during a two minute period.

A cross for the purpose of the competition is defined as the intersection of two lines of the same colour. No Patrol may make more than six crosses in the circle of any other Patrol or at least no more than six will be counted. No one may place any part of his person in his own circle and no chalk marks may be rubbed out.

It is useful to announce half a minute of planning time, when Patrols prepare strategy in Patrol corners, before the start whistle is sounded. Patrols return immediately to Patrol corners on the final whistle.

The assessment of scores in this game is important and several umpires will be required to get it done quickly. If desired the Patrol Leaders can move to the next Patrol clockwise round the hall and make the count in agreement with the resident Assistant Patrol Leader. A table is chalked out beside each circle showing numbers of crosses beside the initial letters of colours and with a grand total of the number of all crosses in the circle. A total is then obtained for each Patrol of all the crosses they have made in other circles and from this is deducted the total number of crosses made in their own circle.

The final score for a Patrol may of course be negative. The figures are chalked up and the mathematicians in the Troop may like to note that the Troop total of individual Patrol scores should come to nil. Three, two and one points can be awarded for the first, second and third.

18. Gladiators **ARS**

Patrols make pick-a-back horses and riders among their own members as considered most advantageous by size. Odd persons left out team up with Scouts from any other Patrol and therefore if there is an odd number in attendance only one Scout will not be able to play though hopefully there could be reduction to an even number by some means.

On the sound of the start whistle horses and riders attempt to dismount the riders of other Patrols. A rider is considered dismounted and the pair is out of the game if he touches the floor or the walls of the hall. One point is awarded to the horse and the rider of the last pair or to all horses and riders still on the floor when it is decided to discontinue the game.

19. Rope Whirl Jump **AR**

A gymshoe or other reasonably soft article of similar weight, is previously securely tied to the end of a light rope about 15 ft. long.

The players stand in a circle about 20 ft. in diameter and jump over the rope as it is whirled round by a leader lying on the floor. A Scout is out if there is the slightest touch upon him with the rope or the gymshoe. He is not however out as a result of a hit following deflection from a hit on another Scout. Only the first Scout hit is out.

In a Troop of 20 or more it will be desirable to play this game in duplicate. 3, 2 and 1 points can be awarded to the last, second last and third last persons in each circle.

20. Shoulder Push **AR**

This game can be played between any number of Patrols but if there are six or more it is better to play in two groups at either end of the hall.

A circle is drawn about 12 ft. in diameter and Patrols sit nearby. Individuals in Patrols are numbered so that as far as possible persons with same numbers are of similar weight. Where necessary Scouts are given two numbers to equate Patrols.

Scouts with a number called enter the circle and hopping on one foot and with arms folded endeavour to push over their opponents or to push them out of the circle.

This is a good game but it must be strictly refereed. A player is out in the following circumstances:

(1) He touches the floor with his non-hopping foot.
(2) He unfolds his arms.
(3) He makes a touch outside the circle however slight.

Occasionally two numbers may be called simultaneously. A point is awarded each time to the last person in or to the last two if they are in the same Patrol.

21. Contra Activities **AR**

Each Patrol is issued with a piece of paper which instructs them to carry out some particular activity for a period of two minutes. Unknown however to each Patrol other Patrols have been issued with instructions to carry out activities which will interfere with their own activity. For six Patrols activities might be as follows.

(1) Entertain the Troop with well sung campfire songs.
(2) Keep people as quiet as possible in the Troop room.
(3) Collect as many gym shoes as possible in your Patrol corner.
(4) Imprison as many Scouts as possible in your Patrol corner.
(5) Keep the hall clean of chalking.
(6) Decorate the floor as widely as possible with chalk pictures using chalk supplied.

It will be seen that items (1) and (2) and (5) and (6) are directly contra to each other while items (3) and (4) are creative of general nuisance to other Patrols. It is useful to be selective in issuing instructions to particular Patrols taking into account the size and number of Scouts in Patrols who will be opposing them. Patrols are warned to keep their own instructions secret and are given 30 seconds planning time before the commencement of the two minute period.

It will hardly be practicable to make a precise inter-Patrol marking of the activity but some Patrols will clearly make a better job of it than others. A leader should briefly give his view of the performance of each Patrol and award 3, 2 and 1 points to the first, second and third.

22. Three Corner Grab **AR**

This game is particularly convenient to be played by Troops having either three or six Patrols though as described later the game can also be set up for four Patrols.

Circles about 15 ins. in diameter are chalked at the corners of an equilateral triangle having sides ideally about 25 ft. long. Another circle also of 15 ins. diameter is chalked in the centre of the triangle. In the interests of fairness it is important that the layout be reasonably accurate.

Patrols sit down in the vicinity of, though well clear of, the corner circles. Members of Patrols are numbered from one for the Patrol Leader up to however many are in the Patrol for the smallest member. If numbers in Patrols are not equal then the smallest members in the short Patrols should be given two numbers to make up to the number in the largest Patrol.

Five pieces of wood measuring about 2 in. cube are placed in the centre of the circle. On the calling of a number these Scouts run to the centre circle and carry one cube back to their own circle. They then return for another cube but when no cubes are left in the centre they take cubes from opponents' corner circles. The winner is the first to get three cubes in his circle. At no time may a player carry more than one cube and no one may obstruct the removal of a cube from a circle. After each round the five cubes are returned to the centre circle and another number is called. Just occasionally a round can continue for an inordinate time. The problem can be got over by placing a sixth cube in the centre circle for this once during the course of play. Patrol totals are taken for overall winner at the end of the game.

It would be hoped that in six Patrol Troops there would be room for the game to be played in duplicate.

The game can also be quite well played by four Patrols with circles at the corners of a square. In this case there should be six cubes at the start in the centre circle.

23. Three Corner Tug **AR**

The layout for this game is the same as for Three Corner Grab except that a rope grommet is placed in the centre circle and an object such as an old hat which can be easily picked up is placed in each of the corner circles.

A grommet is a rope ring which for this purpose should be about 1 in. thick and have an outside diameter of about 6 ins. Basically a grommet is made by taking a single strand from a three strand rope one inch thick, tying a half knot to give a circle 6 ins. across, then relaying both ends of the strand into a rope circle. The ends are tied off with another half knot and surplus lengths cut off. A substitute grommet suitable for this game can be made from ordinary knotting weight rope by making it into a coil of eight loops 6 ins. across and then making the resulting ring stable by tying it round tightly with strong twine every 2 ins. taking care to entrap fully the rope ends.

Members of Patrols are numbered so that as far as possible same numbers are equally matched by weight. On the calling of a number the three Scouts come forward, grasp the grommet and then pull to position themselves to be able to pick up the object in their own circle. A second number may be called if space allows or if it is desired to conclude a contest which is going on too long. A person picking up the object must have contact with the grommet either directly, or continuously through another Scout of his Patrol.

24. Three Way Hawser Tug **AR**

Layout of circles and the provision of objects to be lifted is the same as for Three Corner Tug. In this case however, a rope of hawser weight is tied to give a circle 7 ft. in diameter and set down in the centre of the triangle. Surplus rope can be led away between two of the corner circles.

Three complete Patrols come forward. All Patrol members grasp the hawser over the section nearest to their corner and on order from the referee pull so that someone can lift the object in their own corner.

This game is best played when Patrols are relatively equal in pulling power. If there are three Patrols then three pulls will probably be sufficient. With four Patrols there is one pull with Patrols in all possible combinations of three which in effect means there are four pulls with a different Patrol sitting out each time. For five Patrols one is eliminated from a group of three and the four Patrols play as above. In the case of six Patrols two Patrols qualify from each group of three and the four qualifying Patrols then contest among themselves in pulls in all four possible combinations.

One point is awarded for each win except in the initial elimination with five Patrols. A time limit of 1½ minutes should be imposed with warning of 20 seconds to expiry and no points, to any Patrol for no result. In a closely contested pull a result may be obtained by moving all three objects slightly inwards.

25. King Ball **AR**

This is a game in which all members of the Troop take part together and which has the advantage that those who are "out" continue to play.

Decision has to be made on a first person to be out and Troops may have a favoured means of deciding this. Convenient however for this particular game is that the Troop stands in a large circle with fists clenched. A football is thrown in "fair throws" between players and the first to drop the ball is out.

The player who is out then endeavours to get the rest of the players out by hitting them with the ball anywhere on their person except the hands. As each person is hit he joins the other out players against those still in.

An out-player can run after the ball about the Troop room but he cannot move once he is in possession of the ball. An out-player holding the ball has the choice of throwing the ball direct at an in-player or, often more effectively, passing the ball to another out-player who may be better placed to hit an in-player.

The general form of play of in-players is to distance themselves from the ball. In-players can however ward off the ball with their hands or punch it away with clenched fists or to another in-player. This passing by in-players may be effective in the early stages of the game but in-players cannot grasp the ball or keep possession by bouncing. An in-player is out if, while touching the ball, he is touched by an out-player. In-players are out if they are hit other than on the hands by the play of themselves.

The game continues until one last player, the king, remains in. Towards the end of the game it may be desirable to have a pause on one or two occasions to establish clearly who remains in and so that these players can be seen by the out-players.

This game can be useful as an end game when there may not be time for a game in which several teams have to play each other.

26. Baton Ball **AR**

This game and the one which follows is played between two teams each lined along the side of the Troop room. As contests are between individuals it is important that they should as far as possible be evenly matched.

Patrols should be moved from one side of the Troop room to the other as necessary to get the same number in each line within one or two though it may be preferred to avoid this if it is a tradition that say the three north Patrols play the three south Patrols in some activities. Each line facing inwards carefully grades by size with tallest on right and shortest on left and then numbers from right to left and sits evenly spread along the side of the Troop room. A player may be given two numbers if needed to make sides exactly equal. It is important that the person running the game has a list of the numbers so he can tick them off as called. Some numbers should be repeated.

Goals approximately 8 ft. wide and 18 ins. high are set up at each end of the hall using benches, other objects or chalk marks on the wall according to conditions. Two batons about 10 ins. long and 1 in. in diameter are placed beside each goal and a lightweight football is placed in the centre of the hall. Each team plays from their own right to left.

On the calling of a number the players involved collect batons from their own goals and the round is won by the first to hit the ball through his opponent's goal. If desired a second number may be called to make two a side but with numbers in excess of two a team game develops in which the scoring of a goal may take some time. An element of danger can also arise from batons with greater numbers. Batons must not be lifted above waist height and the ball must not be played other than with the baton.

Points can be given to individual Patrols as each round is won or there can be overall winning by the side with each Patrol of the winning side getting the same number of points.

27. Sack Tug **AR**

A sack about 30 ins. long is rolled up tightly lengthwise and bound round with twine about 6 ins. from each end. Two sides are positioned as for baton ball and the sack is placed in the middle of the Troop room parallel to the length.

When a number is called the players run out, grab their end of the sack and engage in tug-of-war pulling their opponent to their own (right hand) end of the hall. It should be noted that it is not intended that one player should snatch away the sack and both must have the opportunity to establish their grip on the sack before pulling begins. However at an early stage a second number should be called and also quite possibly a third and fourth number. The succeeding players may grip either the sack or the person of the earlier players. The winning side in each round is the one in which one member first touches the end wall of the hall (or some other convenient line) but he must have continuous contact at the time through other players to the sack and there can be a fine decision as to whether it is best to remain closely knit for maximum pulling power or to spread out for greater reach towards the wall.

In this game there can only be an overall win per side. It is a reasonably energetic game which can be quickly played.

28. Three Against One **ARS**

Troop divides up into groups of four each group consisting of Scouts of approximately the same size.

The groups take room over the hall and any three of each four join hands to form a circle. One of the three is designated to be caught by being touched on any part of his person by the person outside the circle. The game consists of the person outside running round the circle one way or the other endeavouring to catch the designated person while the ring turns to right or left to prevent this.

Four rounds are played giving everyone a turn of catching and of being caught with a changeover after each catch or after a maximum time of one minute.

29. Torpedoeing **AR**

This game can suitably be played with old gymshoes which may have accumulated over the years or with bean bags. The number of missiles should be between one third and a half of the total number of players.

Chalk lines are drawn down the length of the Troop room about 6 ft. out from each side. The game can conveniently be played between Patrols on either side of the Troop room who stand along the lines facing inwards with feet in a wide at ease position but touching the feet of their neighbours.

The gymshoes are distributed randomly to Scouts but in equal numbers to each side. The object of the game, following the "go" order, is to bowl a missile underarm so that it passes between the legs of a Scout on the opposite side of the room. Such a Scout is considered torpedoed and out but he only retires to the back of the line of Scouts who are still in and has the important continuing function of feeding them with missiles.

Players standing on the line are not allowed to move their feet or to bend their knees in any way but they can bend forward and use their hands to field missiles and to prevent them passing between their legs.

The game continues until all players on one side are out. As the game progresses it may happen that some players have no one anywhere near opposite them. To deal with this situation the game is halted for a moment while players move along the lines to become generally opposite each other again.

The game requires several umpires watching closely as missiles can come quite unexpectedly from the other side and people may not realise they are out.

30. Time Hike **ARS**

This activity is carried out from Patrol corners.

It is announced that no watches may from now on be looked at and that members of each Patrol are to go in turn on a hike for a roughly equal time but for which the total time will come as nearly as possible to exactly three minutes. For example if there are six in the Patrol each member will aim to hike for 30 seconds.

On the instruction to start the Patrol Leaders leave their Patrols and hike up and down and around the Troop room. When they think the individual hike time is up they return to their Patrols to set off the next member. The procedure continues until the last member of the Patrol returns when the Patrol Leader raises his hand and the time from start is carefully noted by the judge but without any indication of the degree of success. When all Patrols have completed the hike they are positioned according to the nearness of times to three minutes.

In order to cause distraction from the time judging a leader may call out a description of an imaginary hike and talk about the equipment which should be carried.

31. Line Toss **AR**

This is not a game in the sense that any team or individual wins but if well and sensibly played it can be a pleasant change from competitive games. It can once in a while be used instead of a team game at the end of at meeting. The game is sometimes called Rocky Road to Dublin.

The Troop forms up in two lines facing each other about 3 ft. apart. The smaller Scouts should not be all grouped together but have some reasonably hefty Scouts in among them. Scouts join hands with those in the opposite row but with persons one place to the right and one place to the left so that there cannot be separation down the length of the two lines. The game cannot be played very satisfactorily with less than 20 persons.

A Scout at one end of the lines detaches himself, takes a run and leaps to fall flat out on the joined arms. The Scouts who have caught him then throw him upwards and a further few feet along the line. This is continued until he reaches the other end where he is caught by a well built person standing there for the purpose.

As soon as the first person being tossed along the line is out of range the next Scout leaps and the activity continues until all the Scouts have been tossed along the line. Importantly the Scouts who have been tossed take up position at the other end with hands joined across. Shunting back will be needed if the end of the hall is approached.

The weight taken by the Scouts catching and tossing is found to be surprisingly little. It is important that the person leaping keeps his arms and legs straight out to front and back so as to spread his weight and to minimise any possibility of falling through. Success much depends on the Scouts tossing giving an even throw and at least to begin with it will help if a leader calls to get the Scouts to lift evenly.

The activity should only be done when there is an adequate supply of leaders. In addition to at least one person catching the Scouts as they come off there should always be people on either side in proximity to a Scout being tossed. An important function here is to see that the Scouts keep closed up and also that boys are not tossed to undesirable height. Another leader is required to set off the Scouts making their initial leap.

CHAPTER V

ACTIVE GAMES FOR PART-TROOP

There are a number of very good games which from their nature can only be played by part of a normal sized Troop at one time.

Generally these are inter-team games where there are two sides of probably four, five or six players occupying the whole Troop room for a period of perhaps four minutes. Sometimes it will be appropriate for complete Patrols to play each other though if the game is one where large differences in the size of players is undesirable older and younger halves of Patrols may combine and play each other or occasionally purely *ad hoc* teams may be formed.

A game at the beginning of a Troop meeting should foster a feeling of togetherness and inter-team games where people have to wait their turn to play are not therefore appropriate at an early stage. As the evening goes on however there may be a desire to take a rest in proceedings and Scouts will be happy to watch others playing especially as some of the games have quite a spectator appeal.

If there are three Patrols or teams it is suitable for each to play each other giving a total of three games while with four Patrols this arrangement can still apply for the total of six games provided games are short. Alternatively for four Patrols there can be reduction to four games by two games in a first round with following games for the two winners and two losers. Obviously when up at six Patrols there will be less playing time per Scout though if by chance a second playing area is available then three Patrols playing among themselves in two lots is a most satisfactory arrangement.

32. Skittle Ball **ARP**

Lines are drawn across the hall 8 ft. from each end to form Patrol base areas. 4 ft. in front of each base line another line is drawn on which are placed between five and eight skittles equally spread over the width of the hall. The base areas can be a few feet shorter if there is lack of length in the hall.

A Patrol enters each base area and each is given about five indoor footballs. The object of the game is to throw or bowl the balls to knock down the skittles of the opposing Patrol with the winner being the first Patrol to knock down all the skittles at the other end. Self-knocked down skittles count down.

Accuracy of bowling is clearly a big factor in success but there is a defence aspect also which can become important especially in the latter stages when a Patrol has only one or two skittles left. No one may go over the base line but if it is seen that a ball is going to hit a skittle then it is entirely acceptable to throw a ball to hit the approaching ball and so prevent the skittle being knocked down. A well organised defence of this type can in fact be quite difficult to penetrate and it may be necessary to arrange for the simultaneous discharge of perhaps three balls against one skittle.

The directing of the Patrol between attack and defence can call for a high level of generalship and is one of the most interesting and intriguing features of the game.

There should be an umpire for each Patrol and part of his job is as quickly as possible to pass to his Patrol any balls which come to rest outside the base line and in his half of the room.

33. Floor Ball — ARP

The minimum size of hall for this game is about 40 ft. x 20 ft. The walls and roof of the hall together with any fittings and furnishings form the boundaries of the playing area. The game is played between two teams each having between two and six players though a better game with more general participation results if numbers do not exceed four a side especially if the hall is not large. It is a good inter-Patrol game as physical contact between large and small players does not arise and it is not essential that there be exactly the same number on each side.

A strip 6 ft. wide is chalked across the middle of the hall. This is termed the bounce area. Dead areas 4 ft. wide are marked out on each side of the bounce area. No player may enter either a dead area or the bounce area. The game is played with an indoor football hard inflated to give a good bounce.

The two teams position themselves on each side between the dead area and the end of the hall. The game is started by one member of the first team coming as near as he wishes to the dead area and serving by throwing the ball to bounce in the bounce area and then to carry on into his opponent's court. Unless they believe the ball is going out of court a member of the second team endeavours to catch the ball and to return it to the first team either by bouncing it direct in the bounce area or by passing it to a member of his own team who then endeavours to return it to the first team through the bounce area. A player cannot move holding the ball and no player may hold the ball for more than three seconds while the ball is in live play.

A ball coming from the first team cannot be touched by more than two members of the second team before it is returned to the first team. Thus if a ball is caught in the back area of the court then it will usually be considered advantageous to pass the ball forward for return by another player standing close to the dead area. If however, a front player tips the ball with his fingers and the ball is then caught by a player at the back of the court then this player will be faced with the difficult shot of throwing the ball to bounce in the 6 ft. wide bounce area and to carry on into the opponent's court.

Points are gained by the opposing side in the following circumstances:

(1) Failing to prevent a good ball landing in court.
(2) Sending a ball out of court.
(3) Touching a ball which continues out of court.
(4) Allowing a ball to hit the floor or to go out of court while being played between members of the same team.
(5) A player holding the ball while in play for more than three seconds, a player moving while holding the ball, more than two players of the same team playing the ball before returning it. (Note: in making such a return the ball may not be replayed by the same two players of a team).
(6) Failing to hit the bounce area when attempting to return the ball or when serving.
(7) Landing a ball in one or other of the dead areas with or without having first landed the ball in the bounce area.

There is no need to have a particular order of serving and it is simplest if a member from each side serves according to the court in which the ball ends up whenever a point is won. To encourage maximum participation a useful rule can be that members of each side serve in rotation.

The winning score can be varied according to time available and number of games to be played. The first team to reach eleven points provides a reasonable game.

Alert and decisive umpiring is required and it is helpful if a second person can keep the score.

34. Drive Ball **ARP**

A line is drawn across the centre of the hall with lines 6 ft. on either side to form a 12 ft. wide drive area. Again 6 ft. on either side of the drive area lines are drawn across the hall to provide two base lines which separate dead areas from play areas.

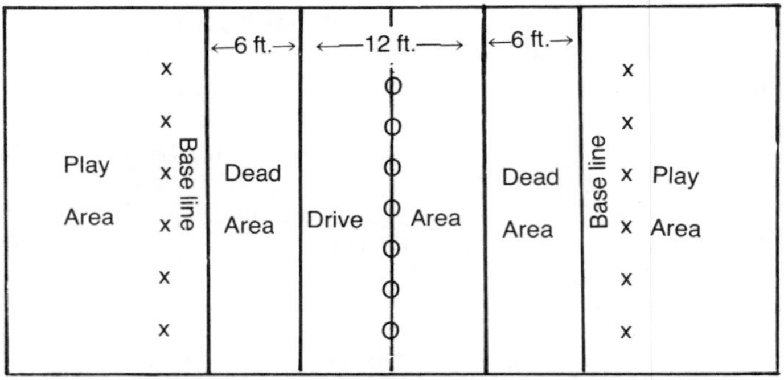

An odd number of lightweight footballs, suitably either five or seven, are spaced evenly along the centre line of the drive area. Teams, which can very suitably be Patrols, occupy each play area and by bombardment with small hollow plastic balls they attempt to drive the footballs into the dead area immediately in front of the opposite Patrol.

Plastic balls are spread evenly among players at the start and 36 balls is a number which allows continuing active play for two Patrols of six Scouts. No player may at any time cross the base line or put a foot over it when throwing. Two ball boys are appointed from other Patrols whose job it is to return any plastic balls which come to rest in the drive area or a dead area to the Patrol to which the balls are nearest.

Umpires remove footballs which have entered a dead area. A football is considered to have entered the dead area when at point of floor contact the ball is no longer touching the drive area including the chalk line. Any football moving into the side of the hall should be moved 4 ft. straight out by an umpire. The winning Patrol is the one which drives most footballs into the opposite dead area.

The game can be played with the small size gamester balls (2½ ins. in diameter) with the slightly larger teamster balls (3½ ins. diameter) or with a mixture of both. The teamster ball can give a rather quicker movement of a football. Tennis balls are unsuitable because they move footballs too rapidly. Gamester balls alone probably provide the best game.

Drive Ball can develop into an excellent team game with some players standing by with a reserve of plastic balls ready to drive back a football approaching the dead area in front of them. Some players may concentrate on bringing forward plastic balls from the back of the play area.

35. Logger **ARP**

The floor layout of this game has some resemblance to drive ball. The game is conveniently played between two Patrols.

A line is drawn across the hall in the centre with lines 1½ ft. on either side to form a 3 ft. wide drive area. 4½ ft. on either side of the drive area lines are drawn across the hall to provide base lines and to separate dead areas from playing areas.

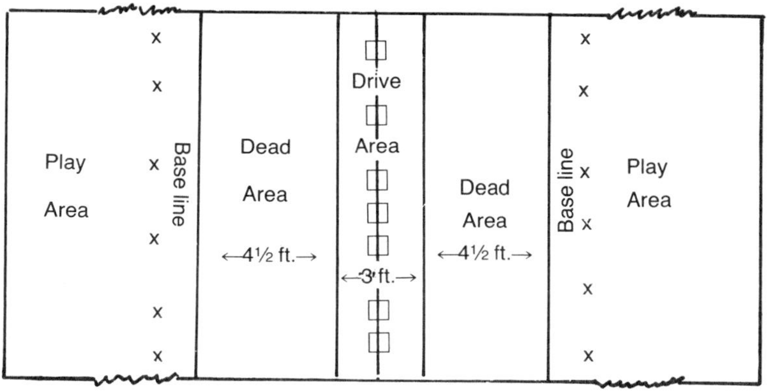

A number of blocks of wood, say seven and each weighing about 3½ lbs., are spread evenly along the centre line. Each player has a small lightweight gymshoe or a rope grommet tied to the end of a knotting rope and by throwing the gymshoes or grommets each Patrol endeavours to drive the wood blocks into the dead area in front of the opposite Patrol. No foot may be placed over the base line.

The intention is that the wood block should only move forward two or three inches when it receives a strong blow from the gymshoe or grommet thrown from about 6 ft. and this is quite critical. For a 3½ lb. wood block a full size gymshoe or training shoe would drive the block forward a foot or more. The gymshoe should not weigh more than 6 ozs. The game will be spoiled if gymshoes are not very firmly tied to the knotting rope. A rope grommet weighing about 5 ozs. is more suitable and can be readily attached to the knotting rope by means of a tightly pulled bowline.

If the wood blocks only move slowly it will probably be adequate to define a block as driven out when the slightest part touches the dividing white line. Blocks driven out are removed by an umpire and the Patrol driving out most is the winner.

It should be noted that the measurements are approximate for 8 ft. knotting ropes. 3½ lb. blocks can be made from two pieces of 6 ins. x 2 ins. timber 10 ins. long nailed together. Separate games can take place at either end of a hall if equipment is available.

36. Heady Handball **ARP**

The ideal number for this game in a hall say 50 ft. x 25 ft. is probably four a side though up to six is quite satisfactory. Although ideally players should be of equal size some younger Scouts especially those good at football are able to play this game quite successfully along with older Scouts and it is usually satisfactorily played on an inter-Patrol basis.

An indoor football is thrown up between the two teams occupying end halves of the hall. The object of the game is to score goals by headying the ball against any point of the opponent's end wall. The ball may not be kicked but may at any time be caught or picked up and passed on to another player. Players can use all their endeavour to obtain possession of a ball without direct play of an opponent. No player may move holding the ball or hold the ball for more than three seconds. If a player has the ball in his hands it is considered "his ball" and other players may not attempt to take the ball away from him though they can position themselves to intercept his pass. An individual may not make successive bounces of the ball.

Overlong holding, improper attempts to possess the ball or other infringement can be penalised by a free throw to the opposing side with all players being at least 10 ft. distant from the person making the throw. In cases of doubtful blame for any infringement the referee may choose to throw the ball in the air. Free throws or throw ups must be taken at least 10 ft. out from an end.

To score a goal the ball must have come from another player and be headed to hit the goal wall without touching the floor, other walls, or roof or a member of one's own side unless his head. It is a goal if the ball, after being headed, touches an opponent and continues to the wall unless the ball touches the floor, other walls or roof or a member of one's own side at any stage in its flight. After each goal the ball is thrown out between the two teams in the centre of the hall by the referee.

The skill of the game lies in players positioning themselves so that by successive passes the ball reaches a player who is able to head the ball against the wall perhaps quite high up from some distance out. The opportunity to develop playing ability can make the game extremely popular and there is likely to be a wish to play the game several times in a session.

37. Push Grommet **ARP**

This is a strenuous but skilful game which can become extremely popular and for which like Heady Handball there may well be a reasonable demand for it to be played several times a session.

The game is played with a rope grommet using the whole of the hall by two teams using Scout staves. Goals 4 ft. wide and 1 ft. high are formed at floor level by chalking in the centre of each end wall.

The ideal number of players is probably four a side although up to six can play in a large hall say 60 ft. x 30 ft. The game should be played with short length Scout staves of 4 ft. 6 ins. and the ideal is shorter still at 4 ft. though a perfectly good game can be played with longer staves. Ideally players should be of similar size.

Play is started by a traditional hockey bully off at the centre of the hall between one player from each side and play is also recommenced in this way after the scoring of a goal. The basic method of play is to place the end of a stave in the grommet as it lies on the floor and then either to flick it forward or as a pass to another member of one's own team or to commence a run towards the opponent's goal. This latter form of play can be skilled as the player moves quickly to left or right and alternatively progresses facing forward or backwards. The effective method of dispossessing a player of the grommet in these circumstances is for an opponent to place a stave under the player's stave close to the floor and to lift the stave or to let it slide, clear of the grommet. At times the sweeping motion of the game can resemble ice hockey.

No play with the feet is permitted except by a goalkeeper who may stop or kick the grommet within an area not more than 6 ft. from any part of his goal. If any other player deliberately plays the grommet with his feet or any other part of his person to his side's significant advantage then the other side may be awarded a free flick of the grommet with no player of the other side within 6 ft.

It is a rule of the game that players play the grommet and not the opposing players. Also, in the interests of safety, it is an important rule that the playing end of the Scout stave must never be lifted above hip height or the grommet flicked above knee height. A serious offender against rules may be put off for say 1½ minutes.

It can sometimes happen that a tussel develops for the grommet with several staves in the ring. The referee should order a bully off at the site, or 6 ft. from the goal line, if it seems the grommet is not going to clear quickly. A bully off is similarly ordered if the grommet goes up more than one stave to a height of 9 ins. from the ground. The interruptions to play described in this paragraph can to some extent be avoided by not having a grommet which is too large or too thick. The ideal size is a grommet made from rope about 2 ins. in circumference and having an internal diameter of about 4 ins. Desirable added rigidity and slipperiness can be given to the grommet by the process of worm, parcel and serve for which consult a seamanship manual.

The game requires good refereeing with the referee being prepared to follow and observe the play closely up and down the hall. Because the game is strenuous this gives opportunity for resting where there are excess players. For example if there are seven players a side then five should be playing and two sitting out by turn in roster.

38. Volley Ball **ARP**

This can be a good inter-team or inter-Patrol game but some younger boys especially may not be able to play it well enough to make it attractive.

It is worthwhile to have an intensive learning session so that a standard will be reached where the game can be generally played and it is suggested in No. 163 that for this purpose the game be played on some occasion as part of a circuit.

39. Curtain Ball **ARP**

This activity requires some initial construction work which is then followed by an interesting and novel inter-Patrol game. Depending on circumstances all Patrols in the Troop may be able to play the game simultaneously. The game is suitable as a Troop meeting end game.

The general arrangement is to put an opaque curtain about 6 ft. high down the length of the hall. Teams are on either side of the curtain in courts marked in chalk across the hall and the game is played by throwing a lightweight football back and forth over the curtain.

The curtain is supported by a framework of tent poles for which the basic lashing required is the figure-of-eight. Depending on numbers required Patrols make self-standing tripods from three 7 ft. long tent pole uprights. The feet of the tripod are close together and are unlikely to slip outwards but a lashing can be put round as a precaution about 1 ft. from the floor. The tripods are spaced down the centre of the hall and are joined at the top by ridge poles either lying between the poles on top of the figure-of-eight lashing or placed on a spike of an upright.

The curtain is made by tents or more simply, if they are of suitable size, by groundsheets draped over the ridges. In order that the whole construction proceeds quickly and smoothly previous thought should be given to jobs to be done by each Patrol.

The number of courts chalked out by lines across the hall will depend upon the size of the hall and the number of games it is intended to play simultaneously. It is convenient for umpiring if the edge of a court coincides with a break between tents or groundsheets. A dead area is marked 3 ft. out on both sides of the curtain.

In order to give plenty of participation four a side is probably the ideal number and if for example the hall is 54 ft. long then one could have three courts each 18 ft. wide and 24 Scouts could play at the same time. However there could just as well be two courts 27 ft. wide with five or six in each team. Indeed if there are only two or three Patrols one could use the whole hall as one court with the curtain put across the middle of the hall.

The novelty of the game is the sudden appearance of the ball over the curtain anywhere along the length and alertness and quick reactions are necessary. There is no need to have any arrangement for sequence of serving and after the gaining of a point play continues by the person to whom the ball naturally comes throwing it back over the curtain. No one may hold the ball for more than three seconds during play. One pass may be made within a team before the ball is thrown back over the curtain. No one may play the ball standing in the dead area.

Since teams cannot see if they have gained or lost a point it is essential that there is an umpire for each game who stands between two tents or groundsheets at the side of the court. The umpire in addition to keeping the score announces how points have been won or lost; for example that the other team dropped the ball or it went out of court.

Points are given to opponents as a result of allowing the ball to touch the floor in one's own court except in the dead area, touching a ball which then continues out of court or into the dead area, failing to throw the ball over the curtain, holding a ball for more than three seconds, the ball being touched by more than two persons before it is returned, sending the ball into one's own or the opponent's dead area, playing the ball standing in the dead area, sending the ball out of court which includes hitting roof, walls, or surrounding furniture or the ball going into the adjacent court. Eleven points is a suitable winning score.

It is important that there is good clearing up organisation after this activity. An easy arrangement is that Patrols take down and clear away the material which they put up.

40. Bench Pursuit **ARP**

This is a variation of Bench Relay described in No. 123 and it is run in a similar manner to trestle chariot pursuit described in No. 64.

Assuming a hall is 40 ft. long, a central reservation is formed by a row of benches or chairs put down the middle of the length of the hall leaving about 10 ft. clear from each end wall. Whatever the length of the hall however, the central reservation should not exceed 20 ft. with any spare space being taken up at the end corners so that the initial separation between Patrols is not too great.

Two Patrols are involved at a time and take up position behind the starting lines each with two benches. A Patrol's own benches need not be identical but there must be reasonable matching of benches between Patrols. Unequal numbers in Patrols does not matter significantly.

On the start order the Patrols progress round the circuit without touching the floor using the benches as moving stepping stones. If any Scout touches the floor then the whole Patrol must remain inactive for ten seconds under the timing of an umpire. The winning Patrol is the one which first makes up on the other Patrol as defined by any member of the Patrol touching a bench of the other Patrol while still in contact with his own bench.

If by chance Patrols are so evenly matched that the pursuit becomes over-prolonged then it is announced that the winner will be the Patrol which is nearest in pursuit when the whistle is blown in 30 seconds time.

CHAPTER VI

LEARNING ACTIVITIES AND COMPETITIONS

While most Scouts probably come to Troop meetings primarily for the fun they get from taking part in games and competitions with friends there is much satisfaction to be gained from learning something new or acquiring a new skill and ideally a Scout should be able to go home from every Troop meeting feeling he can now do something which he could not do before.

A common pattern for many learning activities is that there is first a quick demonstration. This is followed by an instruction period in Patrol corners where the objective is for everyone to learn the skill with those who already know it teaching those who do not. Sometimes it may be advisable to give separate previous instruction at least to Patrol Leaders.

Inter-Patrol pointing is often done by awarding one point to every person who can demonstrate the skill such as tying a particular knot or doing some gymnastic trick and indeed the activity may well lead to passes in specific Scout tests. Unequal numbers in Patrols are adjusted by calculating on the basis of a percentage or ten persons in a Patrol. On other occasions the learning period may be followed by some inter-Patrol competition which requires the performance of the skill.

In addition to the items described directly below there are numbers of other activities which are of a learning type given under other headings in this book and these are cross referenced at the end of this chapter.

41. National Grid NL

A short description is given of the use of the national grid. Patrols then have a period learning or revising how to read national grid references and this is followed up with an inter-Patrol competition.

The national grid system is explained in 'The Fun of Scouting' and Scouts can be given opportunity for personal practice among themselves by the issue to each Patrol of two or three maps on which there is a panel explaining the system.

At the end of the practice period each Patrol is left with one copy of the same map which may perhaps be the local map or a map of an area where the Troop has been camping. This map is laid out about 10 ft. in front of each Patrol and beside each map is a sheet of paper and pencil. Each member of the Patrol is given a number starting with one for the Patrol Leader up to the highest number for the youngest Scout. Patrols are evened up by giving more than one number to Scouts in small Patrols.

A six figure grid reference is called out followed, after a slight pause, by a number. It is desirable at the same time to write up the grid reference where it can be clearly seen by everyone. On the calling of the number that Scout runs out to find the grid reference point on the map and this has been chosen so that it is a height above sea level. There is a time limit which can be 30 seconds or less depending on ability, and all Scouts who have written down the height correctly on the paper before a time-up whistle sounds gain a Patrol point.

42. Knot Learning NLV

It is decided to have a session revising or learning some specific knots. Many knots are shown in various Scout books and in general books on knotting.

After a quick demonstration there is a period of instruction in Patrol corners with lashing ropes available for everyone.

A simple competition to follow is that a point is given to everyone who can tie the knot or knots correctly. This can be particularly appropriate if a knot is being learnt which is new to almost everyone as for example the rolling hitch might be. In this case it would be hoped that all Patrols would gain 100%.

If several knots have been learnt or revised a suitable game is Knot Advance which is intended to develop ability in rapid tying. See No. 95.

43. Morse Code NLMV

It is not always realised that the morse code can be quickly and easily taught to an extent which will allow Scouts to feel they have learnt something worthwhile and where it can form the basis of activities. The use of the morse code is covered in Scouting for Boys and while the availability of some lights or buzzers is desirable to show use over distance it should be appreciated that because dots and dashes can be represented in so many different ways the code can be taught and practiced in the Troop room without any specialised equipment.

In a first session on the subject the aspect to emphasise is the ease of learning and this can be done by setting out the alphabet in the following manner:

Dots only		Dashes only
E •		T –
I • •		M – –
S • • •		O – – –
H • • • •		
	Opposites	
A • –		N – •
U • • –		D – • •
B – • • •		V • • • –
F • • – •		L • – • •
G – – •		W • – –
Q – – • –		Y – • – –
	Opposite Sandwiches	
K – • –		R • – •
P • – – •		X – • • –
	Rather difficult	
C – • – •	J • – – –	Z – – • •

At least a torch with an on/off pressure switch can be on hand to demonstrate the making of dots and dashes. For persons starting it is very helpful if the dots are quite short while the dashes are over long. At this stage it should also be shown that a dot can be represented by bringing down a clenched fist on a bench or the floor while a dash is sent by bringing down the open palm of the hand and that morse can be spoken by saying "di" for a dot and "dah" for a dash. The letter L is thus di-dah-di-di.

The four letters E I S H consist of one to four dots and the three letters T M O of one to three dashes. We can thus learn seven letters which is more than one quarter of the alphabet in the matter of seconds which it takes to make the statement of how these letters are made.

It is suggested that the first two pairs of opposites are also included in a first session because all the vowels will then be known which will facilitate the making of practice words. We are now only two short of half the alphabet.

After this quick initial exposition pieces of paper with the 11 letters which have been covered are issued at the rate of one per Scout and Patrols go to Patrol corners for learning and practice in sending and receiving under Patrol Leaders. It is naturally preferable that each Patrol should have some piece of sending equipment such as a light with key, a torch or a buzzer but it is perfectly acceptable to practice by the fist and palm method. Buzzers should be adjusted so that the making and breaking of the circuit does not cause loud tapping which the beginner may confuse with the true buzzing of dots and dashes.

After about five minutes practice a suitable inter-Patrol competition is as follows:

Lines are drawn down the length of the hall about 5 ft. out from each side. One side of the hall is for sending and the other for receiving. Patrols split into two with the sending half being under the Patrol Leader and the receiving half under the Assistant Patrol Leader. Both halves must keep behind their respective lines.

The Assistant Patrols Leaders are given three sheets of blank paper and the Patrol Leaders are issued with three copies of a list of words composed only of the eleven letters which have been learnt and the object of the competition is for the sending half of the Patrol to signal in morse as many of the words as possible across the hall to the receivers on the other side. Scouts can refer to the papers with the morse letters and are to be encouraged afterwards to pocket them and taken them home.

Lights can be used by Patrols if available but it is up to the Patrol Leader to organise as many sending and receiving stations as he wants to using the fist and palm method. Obviously the more stations he has working well the more words will be got across in a limited time of say six minutes.

Longer words get more points and it is announced that one point will be deducted for any unlisted words appearing on the receivers sheets which are handed in for counting up at the end of the competition. The following is a list of words based on the 11 letters.

1 point		2 points		3 points	4 points
Hot	Aid	Mash	Same	House	Autumn
Ant	Eat	Sham	Emit	Mouth	Asthma
Son	Nut	Moat	Mast	Shade	
Mat	Toe	Some	Tame	Mound	
Tie	Sum	Time	Soot	Steam	
The	Has	Nose	Mist	Smash	
Mad	Him	That	Name	Shame	
Ash	Not	Meat	Dust	Demon	
And	End	Stem	Team		
Tea	Mud	Shed	Sand		
Dud	Hoe	Must	Shoe		
Ton	Sun	Date	Toad		
		Made	Most		

It may well be felt that this single occasion on the morse code is sufficient to stimulate interest in the subject and it should be left to individuals to learn more if they wish. On the other hand it may be decided to cover the whole of the code and this will require another two sessions including the numerals and miscellaneous signals.

In the next session the remaining four pairs of opposites and the first pair of opposite sandwiches can be covered. A learning sheet should be issued to everyone which besides giving the new letters should also have the letters learnt the previous week.

If the subject is being taken this far it is really essential to have a signalling light or loud buzzer and there should not be difficulty in this. After a learning period the competition on this occasion can consist of the reading of letters and easy words sent out by a leader on a light or buzzer which can be seen or heard by the whole Troop. Once again it is best if the Scouts are allowed to retain their learning sheets.

The competition is supervised by Patrol Leaders who move round the hall one place clockwise to the next Patrol. All Scouts except Patrol Leaders are issued with a piece of paper on which they write down the side numbers one to ten. After the signalling has been completed a set of answers is issued to each Patrol and individuals sheets are marked to the mutual satisfaction of the Scouts and the visiting Patrol Leader. Patrol averages are then calculated to determine order of placing.

In the final session the whole of the alphabet with the last five letters in the easy learning form are issued. Also given out are all the letters in alphabetical order, the numerals and the miscellaneous signals. For convenience these are set out below.

A • –	J • – – –	S • • •	2 • • – – –
B – • • •	K – • –	T –	3 • • • – –
C – • – •	L • – • •	U • • –	4 • • • • –
D – • •	M – –	V • • • –	5 • • • • •
E •	N – •	W • – –	6 – • • • •
F • • – •	O – – –	X – • • –	7 – – • • •
G – – •	P • – – •	Y – • – –	8 – – – • •
H • • • •	Q – – • –	Z – – • •	9 – – – – •
I • •	R • – •	1 • – – – –	0 – – – – –

Signal	*Meaning and Use*
VE, VE, VE	Calling up signal
K	Carry on (answer to VE if ready to receive message)
Q	Wait (answer to VE if not ready to receive message)

T	General answer (used to answer all signals unless otherwise stated)
8 dots	Erase (to erase anything sent incorrectly)
AR	End of message signal
R	Message received correctly (answer to AR)

By this stage some Scouts may find it is getting a little beyond them and to avoid loss of confidence the competition after the short learning period should be a quick and easy one. Patrols are split across the hall into a sending and receiving station. The sending stations are given a message which is the same for all Patrols except for the final word. The message for one Patrol might read "Place on a bench (or chair) a book". In order that other Patrols do not just imitate what the first Patrol has done the final word is varied to a readily available object of roughly equal signalling difficulty which might be belt, shoe, sock, coin or rope.

There should of course be follow up with morse signalling at camp in order to make it clear that morse is intended to be used over a distance and the activity is particularly suitable at a September weekend camp when there are long dark evenings to be occupied. Some preliminary practice should be done by Patrols in the vicinity of the campsite. Scouts should have been encouraged to bring press button torches to camp and copies of the easy learning layout of morse code should be available.

The form of the activity will depend on the terrain and the number of Scouts but whatever is done should be simple and the main objective may really be to give added interest to a walk in the dark. It is worth noting nevertheless that everyone has the opportunity to read incoming messages although only one person sends outgoing messages.

If for example the campsite is beside a stream on the floor of a valley then half the Patrols might proceed to a prominent point above the valley about a mile up stream while the other Patrols go to similar points on the other side of the valley. Maps may or may not be necessary. It is explained beforehand that the parties will exchange messages which will be to their mutual advantage. It is normally best if a leader goes with each party to issue the message at the appropriate time. Messages exchanged could be instructions to go to points on the floor of the valley to pick up "supplies" which might consist of an issue of biscuits or even of chips from a local shop. Care should be taken that the wording of the message is such that it cannot be acted upon until the last word is received.

Another simple activity is for a leader to signal from some

distance out an advantageous message into the camp. The message can be repeated several times but is most advantageous to Patrols acting on it first.

44. Methods of Moving Injured Persons without Stretcher AL
Information is given in some Scout literature and in first aid books on moving injured persons and demonstration can be given from time to time of as many as desired of human crutch, four-handed seat, three-handed seat, pick-a-back, two handed seat and fireman's lift. The four-handed seat can in particular lend itself to a relay race. After a period of practice in Patrol corners in quickly and correctly gripping the wrists and in taking on a patient, Patrols take up relay formation (see Chapter XII). Every member of the Patrol must be carried by four-handed seat to the far end of the hall and back though as for other relays involving the carrying of Patrol members a person may be carried a second time as a substitute for a very heavy person.

Every Scout in the Patrol is to act twice as a carrier. At least one carrier must change each run and no Scout may carry for more than two runs in succession. If extra carries are required to equalise numbers these must involve change of patient and of at least one carrier. If there are six in a Patrol it is in order for 1, 2, 3 and 4, 5, 6 to change among themselves in two separate groups but each group must make its three runs successively and not alternately with the other group.

The fireman's lift has a learning novelty appeal for boys and a follow up competition is probably not necessary. A relay on the lines of the four-handed seat is not desirable.

The whole subject can form an item of a circuit (see Chapter XIII) and No. 159).

Once the large majority of the methods have been covered a good follow up competition is a display (see Chapter VIII and No. 80).

45. Tree Identification NLMV
Ability to identify trees is a valuable part of the Scout programme not only from the point of view of developing interest in the countryside but also from the practical aspect of knowing the uses of various timbers and the burning qualities of firewoods.

It is worthwhile to hold a twig identification training session once a year or so especially in winter time when the majority of trees are not in leaf. A leader will need to become familiar with the subject, which can be quickly done, and collect a set of twigs from say 18 different common trees. Care should be taken only to include trees which grow naturally in Britain and to exclude fruit trees or other species normally only found in gardens. Tree identification pocket books are readily available and some excellent concise literature is published by the Forestry Commission with notes on uses of timbers. The following might form a useful learning set of 18 but the number could be reduced.

Conifers	*Broadleaved Trees*	
Scots Pine	Ash	Birch
Larch	Horse Chestnut	Holly
Norway Spruce	Sycamore	Hawthorn
Sitka Spruce	Beech	Rowan
Cypress	Lime	Oak
Yew	Willow	Alder

The particular approach is to demonstrate how easy is the subject. The six listed conifers are all evergreen except larch. Scots pine has long needles, Norway spruce is the traditional Christmas tree while Sitka spruce although similar is so sharp as to be dangerous for this purpose. Cypress has flat fern-like leaves while yew has soft flat dark green needles and reddish bark.

The first group of broadleaved trees can be identified by having buds in pairs. Here we have ash with black buds, horse chestnut with sticky buds and sycamore with green buds.

Other broadleaved trees can be identified in winter as follows:

Beech has long spindle shaped buds and twigs commonly carry russet brown previous season leaves.

Lime has reddish zig-zag twigs.

Willow is recognised by its buds giving rise to catkins.

Birch twigs are thin with very small buds.

Holly is generally recognised by its evergreen leaves.

Hawthorn has greyish twigs with spines.

Rowan has large purplish buds and the twigs commonly carry the previous year's flower stalks.

Oak has small buds clustered at the tip of the shoot.

Alder is mainly recognised by unexpanded male catkins and remaining female catkins from previous summer.

After a quick general exposition it is ideal if each Patrol can have a set of twigs with naming tie on labels for individual study for say ten minutes. It will be announced that there is to be a competition requiring ability to identify the twigs and Patrol Leaders can test the knowledge of their Patrols by displaying twigs with the face of the labels to the floor.

Since trees have to be visited to obtain one specimen there is little extra effort required to obtain twigs for all Patrols though it should be noted that while there are unlikely to be objections to the taking of twigs in the countryside it might be held to cause unacceptable damage to some trees especially in ornamental situations.

Twig identification conveniently lends itself to a relay formation game of which the general format is described in Chapter XII and which is as follows in detail.

Boxes about 3 ft. square are drawn on the floor opposite each Patrol at the other end of the hall and a set of twigs with the labels taken off are spread evenly in each box. In case some Scouts have come to identify twigs in their set by the size or shape rather than by the features of the particular species it is desirable that Patrols should be given a set other than the one from which they were learning.

Members of Patrols are numbered with the Patrol Leader being number one and additional numbers being given if necessary to Scouts to make up to the number in the largest Patrol. The method of play is to call a tree species followed after a slight pause by a number. Scouts of that number run to their box, bring back the twig of the tree of that name and place it on the floor in front of their Patrol. Scoring is to give two points to the Scout who brings a twig back first and one point to the second irrespective of whether the twigs are correct. Five points are given in every case where the correct twig is brought back within 30 seconds. A five second warning is called of the time-up whistle. Only one twig can be taken from the box in the same turn. Twigs are returned to the boxes by the Scouts who took them out after assessment of each turn.

A competition in tree identification can also be very suitably done by the passing round method as described in general terms in Chapter XI and in detail for trees in No. 120.

The whole subject of tree identification can be covered again using the same competitions when the trees are in leaf.

46. Progress in Awards **NL**

Fairly frequently there will require to be a period in Troop meetings when Patrol Leaders can assess the progress being made by their Scouts in the various Awards. The requirements for individual Scouts are likely to differ widely and leaders will probably help with classes for Scouts from various Patrols and with testing.

A stance in a circuit type Troop meeting can also provide a very good opportunity for items of the badge scheme to be learnt and progress to be reviewed (see No. 161).

47. Sling Tying NL

Demonstration is given of the normal application of a broad arm sling using a neckerchief.

It is explained that it may often be necessary for an injured person to give first aid to himself. Patrols are to return to Patrol corners where everyone is to practice on each other putting on a broad arm sling in the normal way but following that everyone is to devise and practice a means whereby they can put one of their own arms in a sling using only one hand and starting from a completely open neckerchief.

After an overall seven minute practice period a three minute period is announced in which everyone is to put on a sling one-handed. The quality of the slings is assessed by mark out of five and an average calculated for each Patrol.

48. Local Knowledge and Guide Badge NLM

Knowledge of the locality is required as part of the Scout Award as well as for the Guide Badge.

Street maps can commonly be purchased cheaply in local shops or may be available from local government offices. Maps should be issued preferably at the rate of one per Scout or at least at the rate of one between two Scouts.

It is announced that there will be a competition requiring knowledge of the streets round about, up to say one mile away, and ten minutes is allowed for study of the maps under supervision of Patrol Leaders.

After expiry of the time maps are collected in and Patrols take up relay formation (see Chapter XII). At the other end of the hall one map is laid out flat, preferably on chairs or benches, but if need be on the floor, opposite each Patrol. If the maps have a visible street key then this will require to be covered or cut off.

Prior to the activity a list of the names of 20 streets is prepared and a copy of this list is placed beside each map. An umpire ideally is required at each map although an umpire can look after two maps. If need be Patrol Leaders or Assistant Patrol Leaders can interchange to act as umpires.

On the call to start the first member of each Patrol runs out to the map and attempts to find any of the streets on the list. On finding one he points it out to the umpire who ticks off the street on the Patrol list and the Scout then looks for any other street he chooses. After approximately 30 seconds the whistle is blown and the first member of the Patrol runs to the back of the Patrol and the second member of the Patrol runs out to begin searching for streets on the list. The whistle continues to be blown every 30 seconds or so for succeeding members of Patrols to come out. It is to be encouraged that members of Patrols discuss among themselves the location of any streets on the list so that they can be more quickly found by Scouts running out to the map and to aid in this, Patrols can have a second copy of the list.

The game can continue for about seven minutes and the winning Patrol is the one which has pointed out the most streets on the list when the final whistle blows or the Patrol which first pointed out all the streets before the end of the time.

Opportunity can be taken following this activity to encourage large scale entry for the Guide Badge. A way to do this is to issue all Scouts who do not have the badge with a typed out form containing headings for items for which locations require to be known such as dentists, garages and telephone boxes and with space underneath each heading to write in locations. Scouts who hand in reasonably completed forms within two weeks or so and who can also show reasonable street knowledge, go forward for the official test for the badge.

If desired this whole activity can very well be done as part of a circuit (see Chapter XIII). This may be necessary if it is not possible to obtain a large number of maps at a reasonable price. The relay race is done by the one or more Patrols in each group during the time they visit the stance and records are kept to establish an overall order among all Patrols. An advantage of the circuit arrangement can be that it gives greater opportunity for encouragement to be given to individuals to proceed to the Guide Badge.

49. Parcelling **NLM**

Parcelling is commonly done very ineffectively and unneatly and this is especially to be deplored when it is done by Scouts who are considered to be experts in this sort of thing.

The basic knot to be learnt is the packer's knot which consists of a figure-of-eight round the standing part of the twine or string. The advantage of this knot is that it remains in position as the string is pulled tight round the parcel. The parcel can be finished off by tying a clove hitch over the short end of the packer's knot.

A leader should give a short demonstration showing how the packer's knot is used and the paper folded. There should be little difficulty in providing a hard backed book per Scout and sufficient brown paper and string should be issued to enable all the Scouts to make a parcel under Patrol Leader tuition and supervision. It is best if the Patrol Leader himself is not required to make a parcel.

At the end of a time limit of five minutes the parcels are placed in a line in front of Patrols. A mark out of ten should be given for each parcel and this can be quickly done if for example three leaders each mark two parcels in each Patrol. The average mark is then calculated for each Patrol.

50. Paper Cup **NLM**

A piece of A4 paper is folded and cut to make a square. Assuming the corners are labelled a, b, c, and d folding then proceeds as in diagrams one to four below.

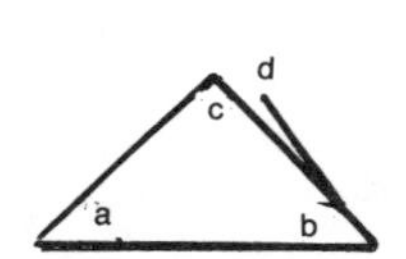

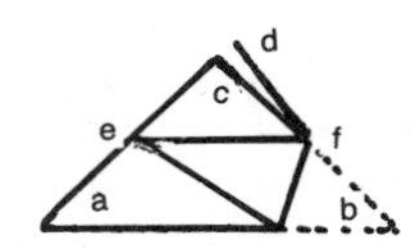

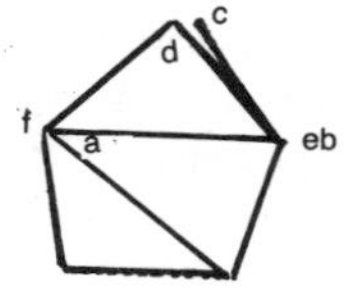

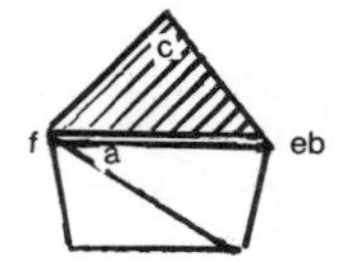

(1) Corner c is folded to cover corner d
(2) Corner b is folded from point f on cb to point e on ac so that cf equals ce
(3) The paper is turned over and corner a is folded to point f
(4) Corner d is folded into pocket ae and corner c into pocket bf

A quick demonstration can be given by a leader to Patrols seated round in a semi-circle including the effectiveness of the cup for containing liquid. Patrols then practice making cups in Patrol corners and here is will be useful if copies of the diagrams and instructions are supplied.

The paper must be of water-resistant quality; good quality photocopying paper is cheap and suitable. Each Scout makes a cup and brings it up for assessment and inter-Patrol pointing. It is appropriate to test the cups by making a serving of orangeade.

51. Rope Crawl **AL**

Whether or not this activity can be done indoors and by all Patrols together will depend on the construction of the building in which the Troop meets.

The essential equipment is a rope of hawser dimensions which is stretched back and forth at intervals across the hall depending on how conditions allow and the number of Patrols. The lengths of rope, which might for example be secured to the upper part of the concrete stanchions of a portal frame building, must be tensioned so that when taking the weight of the heaviest Scout in the middle of the hall the rope is still at least 4 ft. from the floor.

The crawl can be simply done by grasping the rope with both hands, hooking both feet over the rope and then proceeding head first hand over hand along the rope with the back to the ground.

The activity can be for all Patrols to cross the hall without touching an assumed water area. River banks can be designated by drawing chalk lines down the length of the hall about 4 ft. out from the side walls. Also in the middle of the hall beneath each length of rope an island about 4 ft. square can be marked out. This has the particular use of serving as a rest area for the Scouts as they cross.

Smaller Scouts may have difficulty in reaching up to the start of the rope and it is part of the competition that Patrol leaders make provision to overcome this problem by the use of benches and lifting up by bigger Scouts. Similarly a bigger Scout should be at the far side at an early stage to assist smaller Scouts to come off the rope as they get to the bank. It is a desirable rule that no Scout should start out before the Scout ahead has started to leave the island.

Each Scout can gain a maximum of three Patrol points on the basis of one point for using the rope crawl even if not very well, one point for crossing from bank to island without touching water and similarly one point from island to bank. If necessary there can be an overall time limit equal to 1½ minutes per Scout in a Patrol. To equate for unequal numbers in Patrols scores should be worked out as a percentage of possible maximum of three points per Scout.

If a rope crossing is not available per Patrol then two Patrols of more or less equal size can use one crossing by drawing a longer island which will accommodate both Patrols. Once all members of a Patrol have reached the island then the other Patrol continues on to the other side of the hall.

It is very likely of course that conditions will not allow this activity to be done at all at an indoor Troop meeting. If however circumstances allow just one or two ropes to be rigged up then the activity may very well be done as part of a circuit (see Chapter XIII). There is also the very real possibility that the activity can be done outdoors in light evenings either with all Patrols together or if there are suitable trees near to the Headquarters as an outdoor stance in a circuit with other activities perhaps being indoors.

52. Stick Tricks **ALV**

In this activity four tricks are demonstrated using a Scout stave or 4 ft. garden cane. Especially for the second pair of tricks a garden cane is easier. The tricks are:

Jumping through
Jumping back
Over back downwards
Over back upwards

After the demonstration the Scouts have a learning and practice session for about 15 minutes in which they endeavour to perform as many of the tricks as possible. There is quite some satisfaction to be gained from achieving the tricks which can be looked upon as something of a personal accomplishment.

The practice sessions are done in Patrol corner areas under the direction of the Patrol Leader. It will probably be found that only one or two Scouts in each Patrol can perform the tricks immediately or with little practice and it is the job of the Patrol Leader and those who can do the tricks to tutor and encourage the others.

The system of marking is important and should be announced beforehand. A leader is in attendance at each one or two Patrols and a point is given for each trick correctly performed once by each Scout. Each Scout can thus gain four points and if for example there are seven Scouts in the Patrol the Patrol maximum is 28. If there is a total of 12 tricks correctly performed in the Patrol then the level of achievement is 42.9%. In this way comparison can be made with Patrols having greater or lesser numbers. It may be preferred to do two pairs of tricks on separate occasions.

Jumping through
The stick is held horizontal in front of the body with the hands about 2 ft. 6 ins. apart. An upward jump is made with both feet together bringing the knees up close to the chest. While in the air the stick is brought under the feet and to the back of the body with both hands keeping hold of the stick.

Jumping back
From the end position of jumping through, a jump is made similar to that for the first trick. While in the air the stick is carried forward under the feet to end in the starting position of jumping through again without letting go with either hand.

Over back downwards
The stick is held horizontal with both hands palm downwards. The right hand grips the stick about 2 ins. from one end and the left hand

grips the stick about 2 ft. from the right hand. With feet about 6 ins. apart the right hand is placed between the legs about 1 ft. from the ground. The right foot is then lifted and taken forward on the outside of the right arm. Still in the air the right foot is then brought back over the stick from the front and placed on the ground close to where the right hand is holding the stick.

In the next stage the performer goes down on to his left knee at the same time sliding his left hand up the stick to about 3 ft. 6 ins. from his right hand. Using mainly the left arm the stick is taken over the head and the right knee and down the back. On completion of this operation the stick will end up running between the legs and the performer can then stand up.

It should be noted that to complete the trick correctly it is not permitted at any time to let go of the stick nor is it allowed to change grip on the stick. This especially applies when taking the stick over the back when the hands will turn so that the palms are upwards with the stick running across the back of the hand and held between the thumb and forefinger. This may be a position of mild discomfort.

The trick is completed by lifting the left foot over the stick so that the performer ends up as he started standing with the stick held horizontally in front of him except that his hands are in the new palms upwards position.

Over back upwards

This trick is commenced from the final position of the over back downwards trick. Special care must be taken that the stick is being gripped in the correct palms upwards position and to avoid any difficulty in this respect it is usual to run this trick straight on from the end of over back downwards.

The left foot is lifted and taken forward over the stick. The performer kneels on his left knee and take the stick up over his back and head. During this operation the hand grips turn to the unstrained palms down position. The performer can then come to a semi-standing position lift his right foot forward over the stick and stand up with the stick held in front of him in the commencement position for over back downwards.

53. Stave Exchange **AL**

Each Scout has a stave and pairs off with another Scout normally in his own Patrol but there is no reason why an odd number left over should not pair off with a similarly placed person in another Patrol.

The Scouts facing each other hold the staves upright with the palms of their hands and at a mutually agreed signal between them let go the staves and dash over to catch their partner's stave before it falls to the floor.

A line is drawn down the centre of the length of the hall and starting first a few feet away on either side the pairs of Scouts endeavour to make successful exchanges getting further and further apart. The ultimate is to make an exchange right across the whole width of the hall and this can be successfully done over a distance of 30 ft. The skill in the activity is in having the staves absolutely vertical and in raising the hand off without any push to the side.

Ideally there should be an umpire per Patrol but if need be one umpire can reasonably well look after two Patrols. For a first degree of exchange lines should be drawn down the hall 7 ft. on either side of the centre line to give an overall exchange distance with staves on these lines of 14 ft. Scouts who make such an exchange successfully get one point each. Alternative exchange distances may be required in halls of differing dimensions.

For an exchange right across the hall the finger tips of one hand will be touching the wall while the other hand will be resting on the top of the stave standing about 5 ft. out. Scouts making this exchange successfully will gain a further one point each. Points should be equalised between Patrols by dividing the total gained by the number in the Patrol and multiplying by ten.

54. Estimating Dimensions — NLMV

An ability to estimate short lengths, distances, heights, weights and numbers can be a most valuable asset. Estimation of all these items was at one time included in the basic Scout tests and one wonders why there is no longer this encouragement to learn a skill which can have such useful practical application in many fields of activity. The whole subject is covered extensively in Camp Fire Yarn No. 8 of Scouting for Boys.

A very suitable preparation for activities involving the estimation of shorter lengths, widths or heights is obtaining knowledge of personal measurements. After a brief description of the purpose Scouts are issued with rulers or Scout staves marked with measurement rings and paper and make a note of personal measurements which might be:

- Nail joint of forefinger
- Middle joint of forefinger
- Span of thumb and forefinger
- Length of foot
- Elbow to tip of forefinger
- Height
- Span of extended arms from finger tip to finger tip

If thought necessary and helpful for some boys the above list can be issued as a worksheet.

Hints can also be given on measuring longer lengths, for example of the Troop room, by measuring a part accurately such as the width of a plank by a personal measurement and multiplying up. Scouts have a short period of practice under their Patrol Leaders in estimating dimensions.

An easily arranged follow up competition for this learning period is estimation golf. Scouts pair off with members of other Patrols with older members pairing with older members and younger with younger. Each Scout takes it in turn to suggest a hole which might for example be the length of a bench of the height of a chair. Each makes his estimation and writes it down. They then make an accurate measurement with a ringed stave or ruler and establish the true dimension to their mutual satisfaction. The one who estimates nearest to the true figure is the winner of the hole. Nine holes is probably enough at about 1½ minutes per hole. Winners gain points for their Patrol.

Another very attractive follow up competition for this activity is dimensions estimation by the passing round method which is described in general terms in Chapter XI and in detail in No. 117.

55. Estimating Weights **NLM**

While the ability to estimate weights can be equally as important as estimating dimensions the estimating of weights does not lend itself so readily to the use of methods such as personal measurements or even calculation by using elementary geometry. In a session on learning to judge weights therefore the objective has to be for Scouts to become familiar with a range of particular weights. At one end of the scale it will be useful to appreciate the feel of the first class price scale inland letter at 2 ozs./60 gms. and at the other end that a sack containing 1 cwt./50 kilograms is something that younger Scouts may hardly be able to lift.

It is a good idea to choose the learning weights from items which might be taken on an overnight hike and if at all possible each Patrol should have a set of scales for a practice period. During this time the Patrol Leader can test the weight judging ability of members of his Patrol, with such items as a bottle of lemonade, a pair of gymshoes, a hike tent, a pair of boots, a pullover, a rucksack and a portable stove.

Estimation golf as suggested for dimensions will not usually be practicable for judging of weights because of the difficulty in determining correct answers. As for dimensions however, a most successful passing round type competition can be arranged for judging of weights as described in detail in No. 118.

56. Estimating Numbers **NLM**

To be able to estimate numbers quickly and with reasonable accuracy can be very useful. A practical Scouting example might be the number of people in a 100 yard queue waiting to get into a jumble sale.

Generally speaking the method consists of estimating the number in a small section of the whole and multiplying up. Thus in estimating the sweets in a jar one estimates through the glass the number in a layer on the bottom. Then one judges the thickness of a sweet, and thence the number of layers in the jar and multiplies up.

An instructional session on the subject can only be brief and will consist of little more than what is said above but it is certainly worth having. The success of the activity will arise from the follow up competition which as in the case of dimensions and weights will probably best consist of Patrols estimating numbers on the passing round basis. This may take a bit of preparation but if well compiled can be found very intriguing and for that reason the competition and items for it are described in some detail in No. 119.

57. Rescue Line **AL**

It is assumed for this activity that it is necessary to construct a rescue line as quickly as possible by tying five lashing ropes together with sheet-bends and putting a bowline in one end.

There will often be a need for a demonstration of the two knots followed by a practice period of about ten minutes in Patrol corners including making the rescue line and coiling and throwing it.

For the competition Patrols take up relay formation at the end of the hall (see Chapter XII) carrying the five ropes untied. One Scout from each Patrol takes up position in a chalk box about 25 ft. in front of the Patrol. On the order to go, Patrols tie the lashings together make the bowline and throw the line to be caught by the Scout who must not move out of the chalk box. Re-coiling and throwing continues as necessary.

Three, two and one points are given to the first, second and third Patrols to get the line to the Scout in front as long as the line has a non-slipping loop and the lashings are joined as to be unlikely to come apart. In addition one point is given for every sheet-bend and for the bowline correctly and tightly tied. There should be emphasis on the need to pull the knots tight and to have ends from the knots of about three inches. It may be necessary to have a time limit.

Information on coiling of a rope for throwing is given in No. 143.

58. Casualty Simulation **NLMEV**

Casualty simulation has the primary purpose of creating realism in the appearance of patients in first aid training and quite elaborate procedures may be used to demonstrate some conditions and injuries. For the simulation of wounds, only the simplest of equipment is generally required. The necessary materials can all be readily obtained and the preparation of patients showing great realism in various wound injuries can be a very worthwhile activity carried out on a Patrol basis at a Troop meeting.

The following materials and equipment are required for six Patrols to carry out two incidents each with two injuries.

3 sticks of carmine 2 greasepaint (commonly 9 cms. long and 1 cm. in diameter)
150 mls. of castor oil (commonly sold in 50 ml. bottles)
200 gms. petroleum jelly (commonly sold in 100 gm. jars)
200 gms. (common pack) neutral theatrical blending powder
1 kg. putty
250 gms. (common pack) removing cream
4 spillikins per Patrol
8 plastic throwaway cups per Patrol of non heat retaining type
2 wiping up cloths per Patrol (stockinette is very suitable)
One 2 pint (or larger) aluminium dixie per Patrol
One refuse container at each end of Troop room
One bowl of warm water, soap and towel between two Patrols

The greasepaint, blending powder and removing cream are obtainable from theatrical supplies shops and sometimes also from principal branches of large chemists. Castor oil and petroleum jelly are readily available from chemists. The greasepaint is used to make imitation blood and it is absolutely essential that the shade be carmine 2. Any other shade of red will clearly show up as wrong.

Imitation blood can be purchased as a made up liquid but it is an interesting part of the activity for each Patrol to make its own. This is done by warming up a little castor oil in a plastic cup held in hot water in a dixie and at the same time adding the greasepaint. 25 mls. of castor oil (half a 50 ml. bottle) will make fully enough blood for four wounds. Greasepaint is commonly supplied in sticks 9 cms. long and 1 cm. in diameter and assuming this diameter 2.5 cms. is the amount for 25 mls. or 1 cm. for 10 mls. of castor oil. The quantities are not absolutely critical. The greasepaint is stirred into the oil with a spillikin and a realistic red liquid will form within a few minutes. The blood is ready for use when it is just beginning to feel uncomfortably hot to the skin. Note that on no account must the cup be of a heat retaining type.

It will be a good idea for a leader to have previously practised and to demonstrate the simulation of a simple wound such as a three inch cut on the forearm. For this a strip of putty about 3½ ins. long and ¾ in. wide is required. The putty should be about ⅛ in. thick in the middle of the strip tapering down to nil at the edges. It is important to get the edges of the putty to merge with the skin and this is done by the application of a small amount of petroleum jelly. A little jelly will also help to smooth down the whole strip of putty. The next stage is to make the putty skin coloured and this is done by rubbing on the neutral theatrical blending powder. Any powder on the skin should be brushed away.

The cut of length desired is made into the putty using a spillikin or the back of a suitable knife. The spillikin or knife should be slightly turned in order to give a width to the cut representing the edges lying open.

The blood should be poured on carefully starting at the highest point of the cut and allowing it to flow down and over the edges of the cut by gravity. The blood quickly coagulates on cooling. Too much blood spoils the effect.

After the demonstration the Patrols return to their corners and materials and equipment is given out. This can be quickly done by having all the different materials already placed in plastic cups for each Patrol on a tray or in a washing-up bowl. Unless only one or two Patrols are involved it will be best to supply the proper quantities of greasepaint and castor oil together in one cup. It will probably also be best to supply the hot water in dixies for mixing blood and in washing bowls for cleaning up from a central source. Patrols could use stoves but this could unduly prolong the activity.

There will be enough material for Patrols to prepare patients for two first aid incidents. Different Scouts in the Patrol should be used as patients. Although unsightly if got on the clothing all of the materials can be got off without causing damage. Clearly however it is a case where T shirt and gym shorts is the appropriate activity dress. The following are examples of incidents which should be given written down to Patrol Leaders. Two widely separated injuries are desirable to allow Scouts to work without disturbing each other.

(1) Simulate 3 in. cut on palm of left hand and on sole of right foot.

(2) Simulate badly grazed left knee and cut on right arm.

(3) Simulate 2½ in. cut on left side of face and grazed right elbow.

(4) Simulate bad glass wound on right arm and broken left shin bone breaking through skin.

Some fine gravel should be provided for the second and third incidents if it is not available outside. The fourth example incident is more ambitious. A piece of glass should be available to stick in the cut and bone can be simulated by a sliver of wood or by animal or bird bone.

15 minutes is allowed for each incident. One leader gives points for one injury in all Patrols and another leader gives points for the other injury. Five minutes is given for the patient and the Patrol area to be cleaned up and the points are awarded for this as well as for the final clearing up after the second incident.

Including the initial demonstration and final clearing up the whole activity with two incidents can hardly be done in less than 70 minutes. Remarkable realism can be achieved and real distress has been caused to a visitor to the Headquarters and to a parent when a Scout went home without cleaning off a simulated face wound.

59. Square and Diagonal Lashings **NL**

These lashings may be taught in preparation for making trestles which can be used for racing. See No. 64.

60. Figure-of-Eight Lashing **NL**

The follow up for this lashing can be making tripods in preparation for the game of curtain ball. See No. 39.

61. Rolling Hitch **NL**

The follow up here can be stilt walking. See No. 72.

62. Splicing **NL**

It may be difficult to instruct everyone together in splicing and this subject is therefore described as a circuit activity. See No. 149.

63. Circuit Learning **NL**

See Chapter XIII where items are suggested which can suitably be learned as part of a circuit type Troop meeting but sometimes it may be possible for the whole Troop to learn them together.

CHAPTER VII

CONSTRUCTION COMPETITIONS

A category of activity which gives much opportunity for a Patrol to learn to work together and for the Patrol Leader to lead are constructions using staves and lashings but sometimes also other items. This is especially so if the constructions are being made against a time limit. Sometimes the constructions are used for some further competition.

Constructions have to be taken down before proceeding to the next activity and part of the competition will include the speed and efficiency with which this is done and the material laid out ready for collection.

64. Trestle Making and Racing — AIL

This is a well known activity but is usually so enjoyed that it can be included in the programme at least once a year.

Patrols are issued with nine lightweight rope lashing lengths and six staves. It may be thought desirable for a leader to revise quickly the making of square and diagonal lashings and the main points of construction of a trestle with special emphasis on correct layout of the staves and on the need for lashings to be pulled really tight. For this particular activity the ledger should be 6 ins. above the butts of the legs. If staves are of different lengths it is important that they should be issued so as to allow balanced construction. For example, two longer staves can be used for the legs and a single short one for the transom. Patrols can be given say 12 minutes to construct their trestle although this can be varied according to estimated ability.

Chariots racing can be done indoors or outdoors but indoors may be preferred due to the exciting skidding effect which can be obtained when taking corners on a smooth surface. The chariot carries one rider who stands on the ledger with his feet close to the legs and is pulled by three Scouts holding the transom. The Patrol loses if any part of the rider touches the floor or ground. The trestle must not be lifted from the floor or ground.

Indoors or outdoors the quality of the construction of the trestle is a matter for important assessment. This should be done immediately after the first race in which the trestle is used and a mark given out of ten which will be quite separate from any points gained for success in racing.

Indoors the most interesting form of racing is as a circuit pursuit. A line of benches or chairs is placed up the centre of the Troop room preferably leaving 12 ft. clear to each end wall. Starting lines are drawn at each end of the centre barrier across to the side walls.

Two names are taken from a hat and these Patrols with riders mounted and three pullers stand behind the starting lines. On the order to go the Patrols pursue each other round the room. A Patrol wins when a puller, still in contact with his own chariot, first touches the rider or chariot of the other Patrol.

If Patrols are evenly matched, and the chariots are well constructed, the race can be quite lengthy and exhausting. It should be a rule that the rider must be changed after each race and also that no puller may sit out for two races in succession. An alternative is that pullers may take over one from another as relays during the course of a long race.

If a long race is proceeding to excessive exhaustion of the pullers then it may be called that a whistle will be blown in 20 seconds time and the Patrol then nearest to the one ahead will be declared the winner .

The racing is conveniently done on a knock-out system. In the case of four Patrols the two losers and the two winners from the first round play each other. With five Patrols or six Patrols either three or two Patrols get byes into the second round. In the case of six Patrols two losers in the first round can play each other. Two points are given to the winner of each race and one point for qualifying by luck for a bye.

Outdoors there may be a straight race of around 100 yards by all Patrols at once across a grass area. A second race should be held in which the riders are changed and any Scouts who did not pull in the first race are included. Rather more interesting is a race around a course of about 300 yards with Patrol names being pulled out of a hat and each being very carefully timed for the circuit.

65 Height from Ground **AI**

Each Patrol is given six staves and eight lashings and told that as quickly as possible they are to make a construction, using that equipment only, which will support all parts of the person of one member of the Patrol at least a height stated from the ground for at least ten seconds.

In this activity we are not particularly concerned about how it is done and what the rope work looks like. The objective is to get the ten second result as quickly as possible.

It is further explained that other members of the Patrol may assist in getting the individual on to the construction but he must remain free without them for at least ten seconds and he must have no contact with any part of the hall or its furnishings. Also the construction itself must be entirely free of contact with any part of the room or its furnishings except the floor.

The height stated is very important and must be carefully assessed according to the length of staves which are used. Unless there is a large number of staves of 5 ft. and more we suggest that 3 ft. 8 ins. is a suitable height. Umpires are on hand with staves chalked at the height ready to go to Patrols whenever success is claimed.

Points are given, hopefully to all Patrols, in declining sequence say 6, 5, 4, 3, 2, 1 as they complete the project. Complex trestle type constructions usually fail and success is normally best obtained by a tripod made with figure-of-eight lashing, some cross spars for rigidity and with projections at the top within which someone squats.

It may be desirable to impose a time limit and this can be done at any stage by announcing that a further three minutes is being allowed.

66. Wigan Flagstaff **AIL**

This is a self-standing flagstaff intended for use in a place like a Troop room where holes cannot be made in the ground or pegs knocked in.

Material required per Patrol is six Scout staves, seven lashings and 50 ft. of twine for guys with an additional 16 ft. of twine for flying a flag. An outline of the form of construction should be quickly given.

Three staves are made into a letter H using square lashings at the ends of the cross piece. At the same time another three staves are lashed firmly end to end by sheer lashings to give an upright probably around 12 ft. high. A loop of twine about 1 in. in diameter is lashed to the top of the upright as a substitute eye and the 16 ft. of twine threaded through to carry the flag.

The bottom of the upright is lashed to the centre of the cross piece so that the cross piece will be uppermost when the H base is placed flat on the floor and the upright raised vertical. Guys of twine are run from about 8 ft. up the upright to each corner of the base and tensioned to get the flagpole vertical.

The fact that the flagpole can be self supporting in this way is likely to come as a surprise to many of the Scouts. Patrol flags can be hoisted or the Patrol can use dusters or other pieces of cloth as available for makeshift flags.

The flagstaff should be marked for quality after a time limit which might be 15 minutes. It is important that the time limit be adhered to as any Patrol can probably succeed in a fashion if they have long enough and the Patrols which have finished by the proper time can claim that they could have done an even better job if they had continued for as long as the slower Patrols. If time allows the slower Patrols may be allowed to finish but with penalty points.

In this activity the twine should be recoverable. Points should be awarded for the effectiveness with which the Patrols dismantle the flagstaff and prepare the materials for storing.

67. Stave Bundling **AIL**

It is well known that tent poles and staves are often very poorly bundled for transport and the purpose of this activity is to develop packing ability by bundling Scout staves.

Scout staves are distributed equally among Patrols from a minimum of six to a maximum of ten. Also issued are three 8 ft. lashings. The Patrol has 12 minutes to make the staves into a neat, tight bundle for transport.

14 points might be awarded for effectiveness and six points for appearance. The secret is to have one or two staves left to force in at the end and for each rope length to be used for only one set of turns round the staves so that there is not slackening from sets of turns moving closer to each other as they absorb rope running longitudinally down the bundle.

68. Balloon Bombing **AI**

The objective in this activity is to get a balloon exactly under a dart which is suspended at a height of about 6 ft. in the centre of a circle about 20 ft. in diameter and when it is assessed that this position has been reached to release the dart to burst the balloon by burning through the suspending thread. No member of a Patrol may make any contact with the floor inside the circle with any part of his person.

Each Patrol is issued with a candle and with the same quantities of same length staves and lashings which are suitably six staves and eight lashings. 4 ft. of twine is issued and matches are available to light candles as required. No other items may be used.

An item of equipment will require to be made to burn through the thread and this can be expected to consist of staves lashed in length with sheer lashings with the candle lashed to one end. The balloon can be driven into the circle by blowing but it may also be desired to make some construction on the lines of the burning equipment without a candle in order to get the balloon under the dart and to restrain it there until the dart is released. The activity can be unsuccessful with a free ranging balloon in heavy draughts.

Patrols have ten minutes to prepare equipment and each is given three minutes at the circle to burst the balloon with the dart. Two or three circles should be in use depending on space available and the number of Patrols. The activity has good spectator appeal. The secret is to ensure that the balloon appears exactly below the dart when viewed from two points which should be approximately 90 degrees apart.

Attention must be given to the quick renewing of suspended darts and this will depend on the construction of the meeting place. One means is to suspend a rope to a height of approximately 8 ft. from the floor with a loop at the end to which darts on 2 ft. of thread can be readily tied from a chair. In some halls beams may be available from which to suspend darts. Balloons which are accidentally burst should be replaced within reason.

The winning Patrol is the one which is able to get its balloon burst by the dart in the shortest time within the three minute maximum. Patrols can have two goes and each Patrol's shortest time is the one which counts.

69. Candle Lighting **AI**

This is a fairly straightforward exercise in quick and effective tying of sheer lashings.

Two lines are drawn down the length of the Troop room to give a space in the middle probably about 12 ft. wide. A candle is set up opposite each Patrol on the far away line. Each Patrol is given a candle, 2 ft. of twine, three Scouts staves and four lashings and using not more than these materials and not touching the floor between the lines with any part of the person the candle on the far line is to be lit.

On the order "go", Patrols will lash the staves length to length and secure the candle to one end. Matches are available as required to light the candle and the winning Patrol is the one which first reaches across to light the candle on the other side of the space.

It is important to relate the width of the space to the length and number of Scout staves being given for use. It may be thought the Scouts are competent enough to lash four staves together to light candles over a greater width.

The candles on the far side must all have easily lightable wicks and must be firmly held upright, for example, by joiners clamps lying flat on the floor.

70. Object Retrieval **AIM**

Base lines are drawn down the length of the Troop room about 5 ft. out from each side and Patrols are paired off opposite each other across the hall. Lines are drawn across the hall dividing it into defined sections for each pair of Patrols, for example into half if their are four Patrols and into thirds if there are six Patrols.

A foot wide band is chalked down the length of the hall exactly in the centre and in this band in the section for each pair of Patrols is spread evenly along the length a large number of objects. The object of the game is for Patrols, operating from behind their base line, to recover as many of the objects as they can, against the competition of the Patrol opposite, using staves and lashings.

Very suitable objects for recovery are pine cones and 70 per pair of Patrols is a suitable number. Just as good, however, are blocks of wood about 1 in. cube which can be cut from a timber supply without great difficulty or expense but in addition to the large number of small objects there should be five or six larger objects. These might consist of a football, two gamester balls, two old gymshoes and perhaps a packed hike tent.

If one is assessing the competition overall between four or six Patrols it is important that the set of objects for each pair is the same. Each cone or small block recovered counts one, the football and the tent could count six each and the gamester balls and the gymshoes, three each. The larger objects are more highly pointed not because they are more difficult to recover, in fact they are likely to be easier, but to encourage Patrols to institute especially rapid recovery programmes to obtain these high value objects before the Patrol opposite.

The number of staves and lashings given to Patrols is not critical but all must have the same. It is important that there is enough material to keep all members of Patrols occupied and six staves and eight or ten lashings is a reasonable amount.

The overall recovery distance should not be much less than 10 ft. This ensures that staves or lashings will have to be joined to be effective. No other equipment may be used. Care must be taken that people do not step over the base line. No part of the person may touch the floor or an object in front of the base line.

It may occasionally happen that objects in course of retrieval are flicked into the next Patrol sector. Such objects are returned to the centre band of the correct sector by an umpire. The problem can be largely avoided by laying two benches on edge with feet towards each other across the centre band between each sector.

Each Patrol keeps the objects it retrieves carefully and a count is made as each sector is cleared. A time limit is unlikely to be necessary.

71. Pharaoh's Chariot **AL**

This is a simple construction requiring only the ability to tie the round turn and two half-hitches and the clove hitch. Materials required are three Scout staves of equal length and three full length (at least 8 ft.) lashings per Patrol.

The three staves are laid parallel on the floor about 3 ft. apart. A lashing is tied to the end of an outer stave with a round turn and two half-hitches then to the end of the centre stave with a clove hitch and finally to the end of the other outer stave with a round turn and two half-hitches. Another lashing is attached similarly to the other ends of the three staves and the third lashing, again in the same way, is tied across the centre of the staves. The chariot is then lifted by the two outer staves and the clove hitches adjusted as may be necessary to ensure that in each case the side ropes are of equal length.

In use a Scout, as Pharaoh, stands on the centre stave. Four Scouts then lift an end each of the outer staves onto their shoulders and proceed forward. The outer staves become side rails which the Pharaoh can grasp though, if desired, it may be ruled that he may grasp with only one hand leaving the other hand free for saluting in acknowledgement of the cheers of the crowd.

On completing of the chariots by the Patrols they can be given a short period of practice including in particular rapid change of Pharaoh and bearers.

The best follow up activity is probably a relay formation game (see Chapter XII). An attraction of the activity is that five Scouts are involved at once and it is therefore really a team game rather than a relay. Each Scout is to be carried to the far end of the hall and back with second carries of individuals if necessary to make up numbers. As with other carrying games of this type a second carry may be made of a lighter Scout in place of a Scout of very heavy weight.

It is a rule that no Scout may be carried on two runs in succession and that if Patrols have more than five members all Scouts must take a regular turn not acting as a bearer. If a Pharaoh comes off the stave on which he is standing then the bearers must halt until he has remounted.

After use the chariots may be assessed for standard of construction.

72. Stilts with Staves and Lashings **AL**

If everyone is going to make a pair of stilts simultaneously then two staves and two lashings will be required per Scout. If these quantities are not available then the activity can be reserved for an occasion when attendance for some reason is low or it is perfectly satisfactory for Scouts to make one stilt each and use them in pairs.

The basic knot required for making of these stilts is the rolling hitch and if this knot is not generally known in the Troop then the first part of the activity will be to teach the knot with stilt making as the follow up practical application.

30 ins. is measured off from one end of a lashing and at this point the rope attached to a stave 20 ins. from the foot with a rolling hitch made with the 30 in. end taking care that the direction of strain is downwards for the longer end of the lashing. The remainder of the 30 ins. end of the lashing is used to tie a clove hitch immediately above the rolling hitch to prevent any loosening developing from the free end. Measurements are readily read off from rings on the stave.

Using the long end of the lashing a loop 10 ins. long is then formed by measuring off a further 20 ins. and at that point tying another rolling hitch on the stave immediately above the clove hitch of the attachment of the first end. The remainder of the lashing is used up in a succession of clove hitches immediately above the second rolling hitch.

The finished stilt thus consists of a stave with a rope loop the foot of which is approximately 10 ins. from the floor. As the feet have to be got into the loops, as against merely standing on a step as in traditional stilts it is necessary either to lean back against a wall or to have the support of a partner to get the second foot in. Once having got into the loops, however, walking is very similar to that on ordinary wood block stilts.

A variation in construction is to tie a bowline (see 'The Fun of Scouting') with a loop 10 ins. long in one end of the lashing. The loop is then secured to the stave 20 ins. from the foot and right against the bowline knot by means of a rolling hitch. The excess lashing is disposed of by a succession of clove hitches tied above the rolling hitch.

An advantage of the bowline loop method is that a distinctly shorter length of lashing is required though this may not be a significant factor. On the other hand because the strain is entirely on one thickness of the rope there could be a problem of lightweight lashings breaking. Also if the Scouts are not familiar with the bowline they will have to be taught this knot as well as the rolling hitch before they make the stilts.

The Scouts should have a short period of practice after making the stilts. Ability is then tested by walking across the hall between two lines running down the length 5 ft. from the sides. One point is awarded to the Patrol for every Scout who gets across without falling with each being allowed two attempts. Most should succeed. To allow for different numbers in Patrols total points are adjusted to a percentage.

73. Stilts with Tins and Lashings **ALM**

Ordinary rope lashings and tins can be used to make a form of stilts which are suitable for a number of activities and which attract from their novelty.

The tins required are the common food container size with around 14 oz. of contents and measuring about 4¼ ins. high and just under 3 ins. in diameter. Because the tins are subjected to some strain it is important to use the type of tin which has added strength due to one or more bands of corrugation on the side. In fact most tins of this size seem to be of this type.

It is desirable that the tin should have been smoothly opened. Holes large enough to take a lashing are made opposite each other in the side of the tin immediately below the unopened end. A marlinespike is the ideal tool for this though an old large pair of scissors will also do the job.

A lashing is threaded through both holes in the tin and the ends tied together with a sheet-bend to give loop about 25 ins. long. The rope ends are allowed to hang down beside the loop and will not be an encumbrance if they are of approximately equal lengths. The stilts are used by standing on the ends of the tins and then walking by keeping the tins in constant contact with the feet by upward pulling on the rope loops.

Each Patrol should make at least two pairs of the stilts which will require a total of 24 tins if there are six Patrols. Three pairs are to be preferred if the Patrols are larger. Suitable tin cans accumulate at the rate of about three a week in many households. Tins should be thoroughly washed out, the paper stripped off and the tins put in a warm place to dry off. It will usually be best if the holes in the tins are made beforehand.

Material should be issued after a short demonstration and Patrols told they have 10 minutes to make the stilts and to practice for a competition which will involve walking with them. Patrols should be warned that the tins may crush if abused and this may be taken into account in a quality assessment at the end of the activity.

These tin and lashing stilts are easier to use than the stave and lashing stilts described in the previous item and are more suitable for competitions based primarily on speed, especially if the form of stilt is new to the Troop. An ordinary relay is entirely acceptable with Scouts going on the stilts to a line about 20 ft. up the hall from the relay formation position (see Chapter XII), dismounting and running back carrying the stilts to set off the next Patrol member. Only one set of stilts is used and a person who falls off may not proceed until he has remounted which may take a little time.

A competition with rather more to it is for Patrols to use one pair of the stilts to cross an area of ground infested by vipers which can bite fatally to a height of 3 ins. There is also an aspect of speed as the Patrol is being pursued by savages.

Base lines are drawn down the length of the hall about 5 ft. out from the sides leaving a space to be crossed of 20 ft. if the overall width of the hall is 30 ft.

The infested area is considered to be too wide for the stilts to be thrown back and Patrols are supplied with an additional three or four lashings to make a line to get the stilts back after each Scout crosses.

For every Scout who gets across without falling off the stilts the Patrol gains two points though if someone does fall off he continues after remounting on the grounds that a bite will not be fatal for some minutes. In addition the first Patrol to finish receives four points, the second three points, the third two points and the fourth one point irrespective of the number of Scouts touching the ground.

If Patrols are of unequal size an umpire arranges for Scouts of average ability in smaller Patrols to make a second crossing.

Once the stilts are made and the hall marked out this competition takes only a few minutes and it may well be felt worthwhile to have a second round taking Patrols back to their own corners.

74. Stretcher Making Activities AILV

It is intended in this activity that more robust stretchers be constructed than the stave and jacket type.

Each Patrol has four staves, of which two should be at least 5 ft.

long, and nine 8 ft. lashings. The form of construction is quickly explained which is the long staves down the side 18 ins. apart with the shorter staves across the ends and held with square lashings at the four corners. The remaining five lashings are taken tightly back and forth between the long staves with firm clove hitches to form the bed of the stretcher.

Three activities are suggested for use with stretcher on different occasions.

Patient handling indoors

The stretchers are used for a supposed case of internal bleeding for which the treatment is absolutely gentle handling and speedy removal to hospital.

A small member of the Patrol is selected as patient and lies on his back on the floor with an unbreakable saucer with a small amount of water in it on his stomach. The Patrol have to get the patient on to the stretcher and then carry the stretcher to touch the middle point of three walls of the hall and return to their own corner with minimal water spillage.

The exercise must be carefully judged with ideally an umpire for each Patrol or at least for each two Patrols. 6, 5, 4, 3, 2, and 1 points are given for order of completion virtually irrespective of standard. However, in addition a total of 20 points are available to all Patrols for quality in carrying out the whole activity of which 8 are for the standard of the stretcher as assessed by one judge. Points out of 12 are lost for water spillage and for every time the saucer is touched by the patient or other member of the Patrol.

Patient handling outdoors

An alternative activity if there is daylight is a race such as round the Headquarters. It is useful if there are some mild obstructions to be negotiated.

This is a timed race. We are not in this case particularly concerned with how the patient is got on to the stretcher and the Patrol comes to the starting point carrying the patient on the stretcher.

The saucer (without water) is placed on the patient and the Patrol starts off round the course accompanied by an umpire. Careful note is made of the time taken to get round but also noted is the number of times the saucer falls off or is touched by the patient or other members of the Patrol. Each such occurrence counts 20 seconds and the total penalty time incurred in this way is added to the actual time to give a total by which Patrols are judged. Separate points are given for the quality of the stretchers.

Evacuation relay

Stretchers can also be used for a relay game. In this case it is assumed that it is necessary to evacuate patients at extremely high speed due to an impending hazard such as a possible explosion or rising tide.

Patrols form up in relay formation with their stretchers. The requirement is that every member of the Patrol, say a total of six, is carried by four bearers to touch the other end wall and return. There will thus be a change of patient each time and it is also a rule that no Scout may be neither a bearer nor a patient for two runs in succession.

If the Patrol has only five members then someone must be carried twice. Also if any Patrol has a very heavy Scout then it should be remembered to apply the general rule for relays involving carrying of Patrol members that a substitute for the heavy person may be carried twice. Stretchers are assessed for quality at the end of the relay.

CHAPTER VIII

DISPLAY COMPETITIONS

There are a number of competitions which involve putting on some kind of display and these have a particular value in giving opportunity for the Patrol Leader to organise and to lead his Patrol and for the whole Patrol to gain experience of achieving an objective by working together. The first example is described in some detail as regards explanation, preparation, performance and assessment.

75. Gymnastic Display — AI

It is explained that each Patrol is to put on a gymnastic display for the entertainment of the Troop. The display is to last between 1½ and 2 minutes and Patrols have 10 minutes to prepare. It is important that all members of the Patrol take part in the display whatever their gymnastic ability. The Patrol Leader will lead the display and commentate but does not necessarily have to do any gymnastics himself.

It is also explained that 10 points will be given for the quality of the gymnastics done and the extent to which everyone takes part, 10 points for the attractiveness of the display including continuity and 5 points for the effectiveness of the leader and the quality of his commentary. It is a good thing though not essential, if there can be some form of matting available for Patrols to practise on and use for the display.

At the end of the ten minute practice period Patrols sit down in their Patrol corners and the name of the first Patrol to give their display is drawn from a hat. Including someone to keep the time and give warning of approach to time expiry a total of four judges can be used with advantage although if need be one person could no doubt manage.

On completion of all displays it may be thought useful for the judges to comment very briefly on what they have seen before points totals are announced. The whole activity will take about 30 minutes for six Patrols.

76. Drill Display **AIL**

The background story here is that the Troop has been asked at 30 minutes notice to provide a guard of honour for a visiting dignitary. The Scout movement does not do much drill but because of the ability to deal with emergency situations of all kinds we believe we can provide a guard of good standard.

A crash programme of drill instruction in the following manoeuvres will therefore be required: alert, stand at ease, stand easy, left turn, right turn, about turn, quick march, halt, mark time, mark time in front, left wheel and right wheel.

It is necessary that there should be someone present who can quickly demonstrate the correct method of performing these drill operations. After the short demonstration it is announced that Patrols will practice for 10 minutes under Patrol Leaders and thereafter give a display of drill lasting between 1½ and 2 minutes and including all the listed manoeuvres performed at least once under the orders of the Patrol Leader. It will probably be desirable for knowledgeable leaders to go round during the practice period to be sure that Scouts have in fact grasped the pivoting technique of the turns.

Displays are given in a similar manner to the gymnastic displays with Patrol Leaders marching their Patrols about the hall as desired. It is suggested that judges give 10 points for the correctness, smartness and complete inclusion of all the manoeuvres, 10 points for the overall attractiveness of the display and 5 points for the performance of the Patrol Leader including audibility and intonation of voice.

77. Marching Display **AILM**

The equipment needed here is a cassette tape of march music with a clear beat and a sound reproduction system which will fill the hall to loud volume. The purpose of the activity is to obtain some ability in marching as such as against drill manoeuvres as in the previous display.

The following basics of marching are quickly demonstrated: the right arm is carried forward at the same time as the left foot goes forward and similarly the left arm goes forward with the right foot, always start with the left foot, hold the head high and swing the arm straight from the shoulder.

Patrols are told they have six minutes of free scope practice under Patrol Leaders to prepare for a display lasting between 1½ and 2 minutes and the music is switched on for the practice period.

Patrols give their displays marching up and down and round the hall as desired. In this case we are looking primarily for good marching in time to music and it is suggested that 20 points be given for the quality of marching by individuals and 10 points for effectiveness in marching together. In addition each Patrol Leader may in turn take the salute as another Patrol marches past. A few points are given for demeanour in taking the salute.

78. Skipping Display **AI**

This can be looked upon as a variant of the gymnastic display. 8 ft. knotting ropes are supplied at the rate of one per Scout and also one longer rope per Patrol and Patrols are given 10 minutes to prepare a display of skipping.

All must take part even if it is to demonstrate how not to skip though the Patrol Leader may concentrate on commentating. Ambitious skipping routines including long ropes and several skippers are encouraged.

Points are awarded for the quality of the skipping and also for the attractiveness of the display and the commentary.

79. Scout Staff Display **AI**

Uses of the Scout staff was at one time a test in the Scout badge scheme. Each Patrol is given 10 minutes to prepare a display lasting between 1½ and 2 minutes of uses of the Scout staff.

Numbers of uses are given in Scouting for Boys. It may be desirable to suggest one or two before the competition starts. The following is a list of uses of varying degrees of practicability: keeping one's feet while fording a river, making a stretcher, climbing a wall, repelling a mad dog, measuring, estimation, vaulting a stream, keeping back a crowd, making a fire beater, the handle for a camp broom, making a trestle for chariot racing, making various items of camp furniture, keeping contact while walking across a moor in the dark, playing push grommet (No. 37).

80. Moving Injured Persons Display **AIL**

This ability is considered as a training subject in No. 44 where reference is made to six methods of moving patients other than by use of a stretcher. These can provide material for a comprehensive display and for this reason it is best done only when the Scouts have become familiar with the large majority of the methods.

81. Tableaux **NILV**

In this case it is assumed that Madame Tussauds wax works wish to include among their displays a tableau of Scouts engaged in some appropriate activity and would like photographs of a mock up. Emergency rescue and first aid are both good subjects for tableaux which Patrols set up in their corners. The following could be a list of items to be displayed in a rescue tableau.

Treatment of drowning
Rescue from ice break
Rescue from fire
Preparing for transport by stretcher

It is best to give Patrols a note of the items to be displayed. Lashings, ropes and Scout staves are issued in equal quantities to each Patrol. Especially if Patrols are not large individual Scouts will require to be involved in more than one item but this gives scope for added interest in the composition of the tableau.

Patrol Leaders may include themselves in the tableau or not as they wish. 15 minutes will be long enough for the making of the tableau and after the expiry of that time all work must cease. Patrols freeze in their tableau position when the judges arrive. Points are given in equal amounts for the correctness and completeness of the emergency demonstrations and for the overall attractiveness of the tableau. Brief comment should be made by the judges before the results are announced.

A first aid tableau is done similarly and suitable items here might be:

Arresting of bleeding from the lower leg
Treatment of sprained wrist
Treatment of shock
Treatment of cut on head
Treatment of suspected fracture of leg
Transport by four handed seat

Once again it is desirable that Scouts should be involved in more than one item. Exactly the same amount of practice grade first aid equipment should be issued to each Patrol.

82. Letters and Numbers **AI**

These displays are done in Patrol corners. A letter or number is called out which Patrols have to form by lying on the floor. 30 seconds is allowed for each letter or number and no one may move after a whistle is blown signifying time up. A warning of 10 seconds left is called. All members of the Patrol must be included each time except the Patrol Leader who has the option of being in or not.

Each letter or number is quickly marked 3, 2 or 1 for the best three. About eight items are called and the points totalled.

CHAPTER IX

MULTI-PROJECT COMPETITIONS

There are a number of related activities which are concerned with the making of objects scaled down in size for which the purpose is not so much the encouragement of model making skills as such but the development of leadership and the ability of members of a Patrol to work together.

The general principle in these activities is that Patrols are given so much to do that it is quite beyond one or two members of the Patrol to complete it all in the time and success is only achieved when all members of the Patrol are involved primarily as a result of the leadership activity of the Patrol Leader.

For example it could well be considered that an interesting activity is to make Union Jacks by cutting up red and blue gummed paper and sticking the pieces down on to a sheet of white paper. If, however, we issue materials including a pair of scissors to each Patrol and tell them to make a Union Jack then all that will happen is that a couple of members of the Patrol including probably the Patrol Leader will be closely occupied while the other four or five members will do nothing at all productive.

If therefore we wish to do Union Jack making as an activity we must do it on a much larger scale with the requirement being that each Patrol is to make three and with materials issued for making on that scale. There will be a fairly short time limit of say ten minutes. If the job is going to get done the Patrol Leader will quickly have to get three pairs of Scouts working and he may not be involved in making a flag himself but go along helping those who are having difficulty.

It might well be argued that it is not possible to make three flags because although one pair of scissors can be available for each Patrol it is not possible to rise to three pairs. It is also the case that some of the Scouts may not be very good at it and become disheartened. For these reasons the whole scope of the activity is widened by development to a multi-project requiring the making of several items.

Each of the four activities described below give considerable opportunity for Patrol organisation with the supreme example being Business Manufacture. Because there is some similarity between the activities it will probably not be desirable to have more than two in the same Scout year.

83. Object Construction **NIM**

In this activity each Patrol is supplied with a list of objects to be made and issued with materials with which to make the objects. No other materials may be used. Tools such as scissors are supplied if considered necessary. The following is a list of objects.

Union Jack (no actual flag to be available to consult)
Drawing of the Patrol Leader
Paper drinking cup
Piece of fish net approximately 6 ins. square
Artificial flowering plant

For the above objects the following materials might be issued to each Patrol:

Four sheets of white paper
One piece of red gummed paper
One piece of blue gummed paper
Pencil
10 ft. lightweight twine
4 ft. wire
One piece green crepe paper
One piece yellow crepe paper
Piece of cardboard
Pair of scissors and pair of pliers

There should be a time limit of about 15 minutes. The judging is important and can be of considerable interest if done in the following way.

A block of squares each 1 ft. square is drawn out on the floor as shown below

Object / Patrol	Union Jack	Drawing	Cup	Fish Net	Plant
Woodie					
Gannet					
Owl					
Swift					
Hawk					
Eagle					

At the end of the competition each Patrol places its objects in the appropriate squares. One point is given for each object made virtually irrespective of quality. Then two judges, working from each end give 3, 2 or 1 points for the best three examples of each object. The points are written in the squares and totalled to the side.

84. Pipe Cleaner Objects **NIM**

Each Patrol is issued with 56 pipe cleaners with instructions to make the following objects using not more than eight pipe cleaners in each model.

Animal
Bird
Motor Car
Aeroplane
Ship
Castle
Camp kitchen rack for cooking utensils

A time limit of 12 minutes is suitable. The activity lends itself very well to judging as described for object construction.

There is something of a task in taking apart and straightening the pipe cleaners and after the judging the final item of the activity is for Patrols to take down the models and hand in a bundle of their straightened pipe cleaners.

85. Making the Greatest **NIM**

Each Patrol is issued with instruction sheet and materials as noted below.

1. Using elastic bands and garden canes provided, make the highest possible free standing structure. No other material may be used and the only outside support is to be the floor.
2. From one or other of the sheets of paper provided make the longest possible length secured between two drawing pins.
3. Using a match box and matches make structure of greatest possible height. Neither box nor matches are to be damaged in any way and all the matches are to be returned to the box at the end of the activity.
4. Produce the greatest possible length of apple peel in continuous stretch between two drawing pins.
5. In the paper provided find a word with the greatest number of letters. Also find the word with the greatest number of letters

beginning with the letter B. (Tear out words and mark Patrol name on surrounding paper).
6. Make structure of greatest possible height using pack of cards provided.

Materials given out are as follows:

Ten 3 ft. garden canes and ten heavy elastic bands (see cane pioneering No. 157)
Two sheets A4 paper
One box of matches
Apple (as far as possible all apples issued to be of same size)
Newspaper (all to be same issue of same paper)
Pack of cards

The activity is based on Patrol corners and several leaders equipped with measuring tapes are required to act as judges. A time limit of 15 minutes is appropriate but within that time Patrols can make better entries for any item.

3, 2 or 1 points are given to Patrols which make the greatest of each item.

86. Business Manufacture **NIME**

This competition provides excellent opportunity for the Patrol Leader and the Patrol to work together at the same time as it gives a useful insight into the functioning of industry.

Each Patrol sets itself up as a manufacturing company, buying raw materials which it converts into finished goods for sale to a trading company. Finance is provided in the form of monopoly money of which a normal pack will cover the operations of six Patrols. Everyone should be warned to handle the money carefully.

Each Patrol receives an initial £650 as follows:

£5 x 10	£50
£10 x 10	£100
£20 x 5	£100
£50 x 4	£200
£100 x 2	£200
	£650

At the same time a note is given out as below showing the cost of raw materials and the prices offered for finished goods.

Raw Materials

Matchbox £40 (licence required)

Piece of wire	£20	Paper clip	£5
Piece of wood	£30	Match	£5
Drawing pin	£10	Piece of soap	£30
Elastic band	£20	Red pencil	£10
Pin	£5	Piece of thread	£20
Sheet of paper	£30	Piece of cardboard	£15
String	£30	Hire of pliers for 3 mins.	£20
Blue Pencil	£10	Hire of saw for 3 mins.	£40

Finished Goods

Mousetrap	£350	Sailing ship	£250
Catapult	£100	Union Jack	£100
Plumb line	£80	Motor car	£300
Dog comb	£100	Toast rack	£200

Sculptured head of Patrol Leader	£200
Model aeroplane which flies	£200
Knot board with 5 different knots	£300
Rope ladder (10 rung)	£350
Camp dixie rack	£300

In is in fact a good idea for the Patrol to have several copies of the cost and price list so that a number of Patrol members can readily take part in business decisions and several copies will also be required by the leaders who are functioning as the trading company selling raw materials and buying finished goods. Each Patrol is advised to appoint someone as company treasurer carefully to look after the money.

There is no reason why the raw materials and finished goods should not be varied but the raw materials given above have been found to provide suitably for the finished goods and the total of likely transactions can be accommodated within the money supply.

All raw materials will be generally available in any possibly required quantity except perhaps matchboxes. Matchboxes may therefore be restricted to one per Patrol by the issue of a licence though enthusiastic monetarists may insist that it is more appropriate to raise the price of matchboxes to say £100 each. The trading company could then however be faced with an irate company chairman complaining that he cannot get matchboxes to his requirement.

A few pairs of pliers and lightweight saws should be available for hire.

Several leaders will be required to man the trading company and at the start of the competition they will tend to be overwhelmed selling raw materials but this will soon ease off and the emphasis will switch to finished goods being brought up for purchase. Between 20 and 30 minutes should be allowed for manufacture depending on ability of Patrols. A two minute warning of time up should be given and all finished goods in queue at final whistle blast should be accepted.
The following rules also apply:

1. Only raw materials purchased from the trading company may be used.
2. Personal knives may be used but no other tools except those hired from the trading company.
3. It is important to understand that only satisfactorily constructed articles will receive the full sum of money listed. Lesser amounts which the seller may accept or not, may be offered for sub-standard goods.
4. No article may be presented for sale for a second time until all articles on the list have been sold once. The competition should end before significant second round making begins.
5. No value will be put on unused raw materials held by Patrols at the end of the competition but Patrols may make sales of raw materials to other Patrols during the competition for any price they can get.

After outstanding items have been purchased each Patrol counts up its money which is checked by an auditor from another Patrol moving one place round the hall clockwise and totals are chalked up.

The whole of this very worthwhile competition is likely to take 45 minutes.

CHAPTER X

ANSWER FINDING COMPETITIONS

There are a large number of competitions which come into this category. They are usually not particularly active but most give good opportunity for Patrol members to work together. On the whole the activities call for mental skills rather than physical skills. Some consist of solving various kinds of puzzles while others could be classified as almost purely recreational.

87. Shoe Identification **NC**

Without any explanation of why it is being done all Scouts are instructed to remove their shoes and tie them together in pairs or just put them together if the shoes are unlaced. With Scouts in order of seniority, Patrols sit in rows on benches or chairs about 6 ft. out from the wall facing each other across the Troop room with their shoes in a pile behind them. The object of the activity is to remember or to discover, who in the opposite Patrol were wearing particular shoes.

Each Patrol Leader selects any pair of shoes of his own Patrol other than his own shoes and places them on the floor in front of the Patrol. The Patrol Leader of each Patrol then goes over to the opposite Patrol and endeavours to identify the owner of the shoes either by recollected observation or by fitting on the shoes to any of the Scouts in the Patrol. If the owner of the shoes is correctly identified then the owner puts his shoes on while if there is incorrect identification the shoes are returned to the pile behind. Each Patrol then puts out a different pair of shoes and succeeding members of the Patrols go over to identify. The procedure is continued until the owners of all shoes have been identified each time taking care that shoes put out are not those of the Scout who is away identifying. Second turns down the Patrol may be required and winning Patrols are those which requires the least number of turns to bring together all shoes and owners.

Identification made from recollection may be done quite quickly but a time limit may be required when trying on is done which it is suggested, should be 1½ minutes. It may be desirable to have an umpire for each pair of competing Patrols.

It is important that Patrols playing each other are of equal size and there is more to the game if Patrols are not too small; a minimum of six in a Patrol is to be preferred. If there is an odd number of Patrols in the Troop then, provided the need for equal size of Patrols can be overcome, the method is for each Patrol to identify the shoes of the Patrol one place clockwise around the room.

88. Photograph Identification **NCMV**

The need for this activity is one or two photographs of groups of Scouts taken at camps or on other occasions within the last few months. The faces in the pictures are obliterated with white opaque and the object is to identify the people who were photographed.

The number in the photographs can vary from around six to up to about 12 and the pictures should be of a miscellaneous group and not for example one entire Patrol. A leader could well have the purpose in mind when taking photographs.

When preparing for the activity a photograph is mounted on a sheet of paper and after obliterating a number is written in black on each face position. The numbers are then listed below the photograph with lines on which to write the names and photocopies made to a number which will give at least one to every two Scouts in all Patrols. There is interest in endeavouring to recollect the occasion of taking the photograph and to make identification by that means while there will also be attempts to match people in the picture with their known appearance. It may even be discovered that some Scouts do not know the names of one or two other people in the Troop.

It is best if there are two pictures which can be exchanged within the Patrol. All Scouts will be able to contribute to making identification but it is probably sufficient if one answer list for each photograph is handed in for each Patrol.

89. Point Identification **NC**

The object of this activity is to identify a specific point in the Troop room from a series of drawings each one getting closer to the point to be identified.

The Assistant Patrol Leader and one other Scout from each Patrol withdraw from the Troop room to engage in an activity in another part of the building for about ten minutes. The remainder of the Patrols under the Patrol Leaders are each issued with four sheets of paper and each Patrol Leader is shown the point to be identified by his Patrol. The point should be well away from the Patrol's own corner and might be a knot in the wood of the wall or floor or a slight mark on a particular piece of furniture.

The Patrol Leader organises his Patrol to make drawings to enable the other two Patrol members to find the designated spot. The first drawing might for example show a corner of the room and a stretch of wall which will be readily identifiable by some item of furniture or by charts on the wall. The next drawing shows a chart with the area of wall below it, the next a group of three knots and the final drawing is of the knot which is the designated spot. It is not permitted to mark the designated spot on a drawing in any way.

At the expiry of the ten minute time limit Patrols return to their Patrol corners. The Scouts who have been out of the Troop room return and are given the set of drawings from their own Patrol. Working together the Assistant Patrol Leader and the Scout endeavour to find the spot as quickly as possible and to point it out to an umpire.

It can be difficult for one leader to remember several points and to keep in touch with the search of a large number of Patrols a leader is wanted for every two Patrols. Points can be given for speed of finding. The search should not take long and Patrols can watch from their corners.

90. Kim's Game **NC**

This excellent activity is no longer part of the Award requirements, but it can be played in the following manner as a good inter-Patrol competition.

The former test required the remembering of 16 out of 24 assorted articles after observation for one minute. Each Patrol assembles in its Patrol corner a Kim's Game of 24 different items of dress or other articles which they have on their person or which are available in Patrol corners. The articles are well spread out within a defined chalked area and kept covered from general view by anoraks or coats or possibly small ground sheets or bits of polythene supplied by the Troop. A time limit of four minutes should be given for the preparation of the Kim's Games and it should be said that Patrols must not go outside Patrol areas to obtain items.

When all the Kim's games are ready Patrols move round the hall one place clockwise but with the Patrol Leader staying in his own corner. The Patrol Leader then conducts a Kim's Game competition for the visiting Patrol uncovering the articles and allowing the Scouts to look at them for one minute before putting the cover on again.

Each Scout does the competition independently. He must have a pencil and is provided with a sheet of paper on which he writes down as many articles as he can remember in four minutes. The articles are uncovered again and the sheets marked. Two and one Patrol points may be earned by the individual Scouts with most correct in the whole Troop but much more importantly each Patrol with the Patrol Leader who has been supervising their competition work out the average Patrol score and it is on this that Patrol points are mainly based.

91. Pelmanism **NCM**

A pack of cards is required for each Patrol for this very good variety of Kim's Game.

Patrols are re-located as may be necessary so that Patrols of equal size are as far as possible opposite each other. All Patrols then divide into halves (but unequalness due to odd numbers does not matter), one half being under the Patrol Leader and the other one under the Assistant Patrol Leader. Half Patrols then exchange with the Patrol opposite so that half Patrols under the Patrol Leaders are placed to play each other on one side of the hall and half Patrols under Assistant Patrol Leaders play each other on the other side.

Half Patrols sit facing each other in lines about 6 ft. apart and the cards are dealt out randomly face down in the space between. The Patrol Leaders or Assistant Patrol Leaders lift cards and the highest value indicates which side starts. Ace counts high.

The object of the game is to obtain the maximum number of pairs of cards by number or face. The first member of the starting Patrol turns one card up and then another and leaves them both lying for five seconds so that everyone can see the faces clearly. Assuming they do not carry the same number or face the player turns the cards back carefully into their original positions. The first player of the other side similarly lifts two cards and replaces them assuming they are not pairs. Succeeding players on either side play alternately and it is most important that playing order on both sides is strictly adhered to.

The position of numbers of cards will quickly become known and a player will soon succeed in turning up a pair. When a pair is obtained the successful player picks up the cards and passes them to his Patrol Leader or Assistant Patrol Leader. On success in obtaining a pair the side receives a second turn but it must be noted that this is not taken by the Scout who obtained the first pair but by the next player in order in the Patrol. Further extra turns continue to be given if more pairs are obtained with the playing order in the Patrol continuing to be observed. The purpose of this procedure is to maximise the spread of participation. It is always the next Scout in the playing sequence who plays irrespective of whether he is playing a first turn or an extra turn.

The number of pairs gained by half Patrols are counted at the end of the game and these are added together to give Patrol totals. In cases of an odd number of Patrols half Patrols can move one place clockwise round the hall.

92. Premises in Streets **NCM**

The objective of this activity is to test knowledge of shops and other premises in selected lengths of streets.

In order that all Scouts in Patrols will be occupied three distinct street lengths should be chosen which is likely to mean that boys will work singly or in pairs. On this basis each Patrol will receive three sheets of paper of which for example the heading on one sheet might be "List in order the names and types of shops and other premises in Station Road from McLeod's store to the Clydesdale Bank."

It should be said in general explanation that in addition to shops the list is to include banks, building societies and any other premises such as offices and private residences. It may be desirable also to state that only the ground floor of premises is to be covered. Patrol names are to be put at the top of each sheet in space provided and a time limit of ten minutes is given.

The activity can be found quite difficult and about 12 items in each length of street is usually sufficient. Accurate lists must be available for marking which has to take into account both correctness of descriptions and correctness of order.

93. Kim's Game Shapes **NC**

Scouts in Patrols are seated around a blackboard or other board surface in which a leader draws in succession 16 simple shapes. Each shape is allowed to be viewed for about seven seconds before being rubbed out and the next one drawn. On completion of the drawings Patrols return to Patrol corners where the object is to draw all the shapes on a sheet of paper in a period of five minutes.

In order to create a Patrol competition to which all Scouts are contributing it is best if it is arranged at the beginning that each Patrol operates in two sections one under the Patrol Leader and one under the Assistant Patrol Leader and that two separate entries are to be made. Patrols are assessed by total points of the two entries.

It is essential that an original copy of the shapes be available for drawing and marking. It is announced that there may be no more than 16 drawings per entry. Suitable shapes might be as follows:

> Equilateral triangle, square, square with circle inside, kite, circle, circle round equilateral triangle, dot, rectangle, circle inside equilateral triangle, square with cross on top (ordnance survey sign for church with tower), circle with two diameters at right angles, square with one diagonal, right-angled triangle, circle with cross on top (ordnance survey sign for church with spire), circle with small circle in middle (Scout sign for I have gone home), cross (ordnance survey sign for church without tower or spire).

94. Island Description **NCV**

This activity can be used either solely as a test of map drawing and conventional signs or as a map test combined with a form of Kim's Game.

It may well be thought advisable to give opportunity for brush up on conventional signs by saying that an activity will require knowledge of these and issuing ordnance survey maps at the rate of two or three per Patrol for study for about five minutes reminding people that a key to conventional signs is given on the map in a separate panel. It is important that all maps should have features represented in the same way and in this instance it is assumed that maps in the 1:50 000 series are being used. At this stage also the need for correct folding of maps can be stressed and the maps examined for this as they are collected from Patrols.

In order to maximise participation, Patrols divide into two or three sections and each section has a sheet of A4 paper. A description of a probably imaginary island is then read out. If the activity is intended to involve only mapping then each feature is read out twice and a short time given for it to be drawn in by Patrol sections.

Maps are collected immediately after the drawing in of the last item. On the other hand if it is intended to involve also a memory aspect the whole description is read through slowly twice without any drawing or note taking being allowed. Patrol sections then have about eight minutes to draw a map of the island from memory. An advantage of the memory form is that while one Scout in each section may tend to do the drawing all are involved in remembering items and passing them on to him. A less extensive description is appropriate when it is being remembered.

It is announced at the beginning of the description that the top of the sheet of paper is north and that the scale is 1¼ ins. equal to one mile. The following is a suggested description. Items asterisked should probably be left out if the whole description is being committed to memory.

> "The island is approximately 6 miles long and 3½ miles wide with a bay about 1½ miles wide and 1 mile deep in the centre of the east side.
>
> At the southern end of the bay is a pier.
>
> An unfenced minor road runs westwards from the pier to a village of eight houses on the west side of the island.
>
> *Immediately to the north of the road and running parallel with it is an area of marsh 1 mile long and ¼ of a mile wide.
>
> In the north of the island is a hill 380 metres high which is much steeper on the north side than elsewhere.
>
> *There are cliffs on the north side of the hill.
>
> The south-east corner of the island is occupied by a plantation of spruce.
>
> *On the northern-most point of the island is a lighthouse.
>
> A strip of alder and oak trees run along the northern edge of the bay for about half a mile.
>
> There is a church with a tower a quarter of a mile north-west of the pier.
>
> A footpath runs from the pier to the church.
>
> *Just to the south of the road is a site of antiquity."

The maps must be objectively marked with points being given for correct inclusion of each item listed. The winning Patrol is the one with the best average of marks for its maps.

95. Knot Advance **NCV**

This game can suitably follow a session of knot revision or knot learning. See No. 42.

Each Scout has a knotting rope and all stand in Patrols facing inwards on base lines drawn the length of the hall about 5 ft. out from each side. Another six or so lines are drawn 6 ins. to a foot apart drawn the length of the hall in front of the base lines though it may be possible to avoid the whole operation of line drawing by using the lines between floor boards and in this case it does not matter particularly if the boards are rather less than 6 ins. wide.

A maximum time is announced for the tying of a particular knot as in the following example. "You have 20 seconds to tie a (pause) sheet-bend." As soon as Scouts have tied the knot they drop it to the floor. A whistle is blown at the end of the 20 seconds after which no more ropes may be dropped. The knots which have been dropped are quickly inspected and Scouts who have tied them correctly within the time limit move forward one line or floorboard.

Times allowed and knots chosen will depend on the knotting ability of the Scouts. There is not a need to have more than three or four knots as skill can be tested by reducing time limits.

If it is desired to include the clove hitch and round turn and two half hitches then the call for these knots takes the form, "You have 25 seconds to tie round your ankle a round turn and two half hitches." For these knots completion is indicated by the Scouts leaving go of the rope and standing erect.

After about six calls there is careful assessment of score. Points may be given for two Scouts who have advanced the furthest but the main Patrol points are gained from the order of scores as calculated for the average number of lines advanced by all Scouts in each Patrol.

96. Similar Pictures NCM

It is a common form of competition in magazines and quiz books to print two pictures which at first sight appear identical but which have perhaps 12 minor differences which have to be found. This makes a good inter-Patrol competition.

In order that there will be full participation by all members of the Patrol it is essential that the pictures be reproduced so that they can be given to every Scout. Although everyone is looking for differences only one set of answers is handed in per Patrol, the method being that Scouts report differences to their Patrol Leader who marks them with a circle on one of his pictures.

In this way one lot of pictures per Patrol is marked and the rest can be collected in and stored for future use. It is usual for a set of answers to be published and the number of differences ringed is not allowed to exceed by more than four the number of actual differences for the reason that all differences are likely to be found if enough attempts are made and a huge number of supposed differences would be difficult to judge.

About seven minutes is long enough for the competition and Patrols can be very absorbed for that period. The activity is sufficiently popular to be held two or three times a year with different pictures.

97. Leader Description NCS

At a Troop meeting when subscriptions or other money is being collected in it is announced that the money and a particular leader have disappeared. Each Patrol is required to write down from memory a description of the leader to be given to the police in five minutes time.

In order to keep all members of Patrols more fully occupied it can be an improvement to say that two leaders have disappeared and Patrols can then operate in half sections to complete two descriptions in the same time.

98. Round the Hall Naming NCS

This is a quiet type game which can be quickly organised. No equipment is required and the time for playing is completely variable.

Patrols are positioned in Patrol corners and the object of the game is to be able to produce names under a particular heading longer than any other Patrol.

For example the heading might be States of the United States of America. A Patrol is indicated to start and calls out loudly the name of a State. This is followed by the Patrol next clockwise round the hall calling out a different State and Patrols follow in succession with the first Patrol starting off further rounds.

Patrols are out if they call a State which has already been given or if they are unable to give a State before the end of a count of ten seconds. The game continues until only one Patrol remains in.

The starting Patrol should be changed for each new heading. Other possible headings are:

Trees which normally grow in Britain
Birds which are found in Britain
English counties
British wild mammals

Some care may be necessary to define beforehand each heading. It is a good rule to state that variants may not be given. For example if in a birds heading the name gull is called either on its own or as part of a name such as herring gull then no more names may be called including the word gull. The same can apply to trees and mammals and in this latter case it is best to exclude mammals which are sea dwelling.

99. Prince of Wales Slipper **NC**

Scouters will probably be familiar with this game, or with variations of it such as Priest of the Parish, as a party item. The game however can be used as an interesting inter-Patrol competition by development as now described.

The Scouts sit round in a semi-circle with members of Patrols inter-mixed and are numbered clockwise. Scouts in each Patrol then hold up their hands in turn. They give their numbers and the average position to one decimal place is calculated for each Patrol.

The game is based upon the correct repetition between two players of the following discourse which is given below with example numbers. The discourse is started by a leader.

Leader:	The Prince of Wales has lost his slipper and No. 8 has found it
No. 8	I, sir ?
Leader:	Yes you, sir.
No. 8:	Not I, sir.
Leader:	Then who, sir?
No. 8:	No. 4, sir.
No. 4:	I, sir?

The discourse is continued between numbers 8 and 4 who then transfers it to another number and No. 8 drops out. If there is the slightest error or hesitation in the wording then the discourse ceases and the person at fault goes to the bottom end of the semi-circle and everyone who was below him moves up one place to the right although still retaining their original numbers.

The game is re-started by the leader or by the Scout making a mistake with the full wording: "The Prince of Wales has lost his slipper . . ." An advantage of a leader re-starting the game is that he may be able to bring in Scouts whose numbers have not been called. To avoid any undue repetition of numbers it is a desirable rule that no number may be called again without the intervention of at least three turns. Breach of this rule is a fault resulting in relegation to end position.

Although the wording may be complicated for some Scouts at the beginning speed can rapidly build up. Inflections in the voice of surprise, accusation and indignation should be encouraged.

After sufficient play everyone is told to forget his original number. The semi-circle is then re-numbered clockwise and the average position for each Patrol is calculated as at the beginning of the game. The winning Patrol is the one which shows the largest improvement in its average position.

If total numbers exceed 18 the game should be played in duplicate in two semi-circles at either end of the hall.

100. Puzzles and Quizzes **NCMV**

Sometimes an inter-Patrol competition can attractively take the form of getting answers to a puzzle or a quiz. The important thing is that sufficient copies are available to enable all members of Patrols to contribute.

Reference is made to sources for material for competitions of this kind under No. 197 where the use of puzzles and quizzes on a large scale is described as a wet weather activity in camp.

101. Slide Identifications **NCMV**

Various competitions can be run in connection with the showing of slides.

In particular the Curtis Film Company, Deepdale Road, Fleetwood, FY7 6TY (Fleetwood 4697) have produced sets of QUIZSLIDES which are concerned with recognising objects taken from unusual angles and with testing memory and powers of observation.

The slides can be projected to be seen by the whole Troop grouped in Patrols. Time is allowed between slides for Patrols to consult quietly among themselves and to write down the answer.

102. Noughts and Crosses **NCV**

A square 9 ft. by 9ft. is drawn on the floor between two Patrols and divided into a block of nine squares each 3 ft. by 3 ft.

With each Patrol taking it in turn to start normal noughts and crosses is played by placing Patrol members in the squares. The game can be played by individual Scouts or on the basis of Patrol opinion.

In fact ordinary noughts and crosses in this form may well be considered a rather trivial game and a blindfold version is likely to be preferred as having more to it.

In this case the squares are numbered in a systematic way from one to nine. A Scout from each Patrol is blindfolded and sits on a chair clear of his Patrol and about 4 ft. from the block of squares. As the players call numbers Scouts from their Patrols move out and stand in the squares. If a player calls a number which is already occupied the umpire states this and the player calls another number. An alternative rule in these circumstances, leading to quicker games, is that the player loses his turn. The umpire must make sure that numbers are called out sufficiently loudly and if need be repeat the numbers himself.

Another more novel form of noughts and crosses is described below under the name Periwinkle.

103. Periwinkle **NCV**

This game is reverse noughts and crosses with the winner being the player who first forces his opponent to make a line of three. Squares are set out and play proceeds as described for noughts and crosses.

The game is not commonly known and at least on the first occasion it is likely to be found intriguing by the Scouts. At least on the first occasion also it will not be necessary to play a blindfold version.

104. Finger-Print Identification **NCM**

Each Patrol is issued with an inked stamping pad and two pieces of card measuring about 3½ ins. by 2½ ins. with a piece of paper for practice for each Scout.

The final form of the activity is not explained at this stage and everyone is told they will have to make two prints as nearly as possible identical. After practice each Scout makes a print with the same finger of the same hand on each of his pieces of card and writes his name on the back of the cards. The cards are then separately collected to form two complete sets.

Both sets are shuffled and one set with print showing is pinned to the wall at eye level well spaced out round the hall. If it is not practicable to pin cards to the walls cards can be pinned to the floor round the perimeter.

From the other set each Scout is issued with one card and a drawing pin. On receiving this card the Scout writes his own name beside the print although of course it is most unlikely to be his own print. He then takes the print round the room and attempts to match it to one of the prints already pinned to the wall. When he has decided which print on the wall is the pair of the one he holds he pins the card with which he has been issued immediately below the one on the wall or inwards from it if it is on the floor. It should be noted that it is perfectly acceptable for several persons to attempt to match to the same card by pinning their cards one on top of another.

The activity is marked by seeing if the pairs of cards pinned to the wall or floor have the same name on the back and Patrol points are awarded to Scouts who have been successful as indicated by the name on the front of the lower card.

The identification process is not easy and where numbers are large the choice can be restricted by for example three Patrols using a green inked pad and three Patrols a blue inked pad.

105. Footprint Identification **NC**

This activity is carried out in a manner similar to that described above for finger-prints. But in this case each Scout makes two prints of the same foot by carefully drawing with a pencil round his foot placed on a piece of foolscap sized paper.

Named sets are collected in and one pinned up and one issued to the Scouts with drawing pins in the same way as the finger-print cards.

Footprint identification is rather easier than the finger-print but if thought necessary the choice can be reduced by half of the Patrols using a different colour of paper.

106. Potato Prints **NCM**

Inked stamping pads, pieces of card approximately 3½ ins. by 2½ ins. and paper for practice are required for this activity as for finger-print identification (No. 104). In addition a half of a medium sized potato is issued for each Scout. The objective is to make imitation rubber stamps.

A reasonably sharp pocket knife is a suitable tool and the previous week the Scouts can be advised that pocket knives should be brought for an activity (not disclosed) the following week. As a further attraction it is said that the knives must be sharp and that sharpening facilities will be available.

The first stage of the activity is to demonstrate the effectiveness of a really sharp knife by easy cutting of twine and paper and it would be hoped that a carborundum and an oilstone per Patrol could be obtained for quick sharpening up of knives.

Some suitable spare knives can probably be available for those who do not bring them. An alternative is to use old razor blades which produce most clean slicing of the potato. The reaction against possibly cutting oneself can be expected to induce a particular wariness against accident which can be reinforced by instituting a safety procedure of counting the blades out and counting the blades back when a Patrol gets an issue of blades and returns them.

It is best to keep the stamps simple for most of the Scouts using letters such as E, F, H, M, N, and X which can be cut in straight lines and need no hollowing out. A competition can be for each Patrol to produce stamps of these six letters with each Scout producing at least one letter. If there are more than six Scouts in any Patrol duplicate letters are produced with the mark for the best one only counting.

If it is thought that two members of Patrols could do something more skilled then N and X are omitted and instead they produce a Scout badge and a stamp for forging a document to escape from a prison camp.

The prints are laid out in a row in front of each Patrol and judges quickly run around giving points out of five for the particular letters they are marking.

107. Sound Identifications **NCM**

In earlier days this activity was usually put over with some difficulty and with considerable limitations by the leaders making sounds for identification behind a screen such as a tent held up in the hall by some makeshift means.

The general availability nowadays of a cassette recorder allows a set of more interesting sounds to be recorded and readily presented to the Troop for identification. About 12 sounds will be sufficient and each sound, which should be repeated a few times if it is short, should be preceeded on the tape by the announcement of a number in the phrase "sound number . . ." Afterwards there should be the announcement "sound ends." The following are sounds which might be included:

(1) Putting out milk bottles
(2) Sawing wood
(3) Putting key in lock and turning key
(4) Using electric razor
(5) Pouring water
(6) Lighting match
(7) Using vacuum cleaner
(8) Telephone dialling
(9) Brushing shoes
(10) Counting money
(11) Eating apple
(12) Hammering in nails

The activity can well be done by the Troop sitting in Patrols round a cassette player well turned up. The player is stopped after the end of each sound to allow the Patrol to consult among themselves and to write down an answer against a number on a sheet of paper which is marked at the end of the activity.

The activity doe not take long and alternatively it can be done by one or two Patrols at a time in a circuit where a stance requires something extra to complete the time available (see Chapter XIII and No. 164).

108. Sandpaper Coarseness **NCM**

This activity provides a means for Scouts to test their ability to use their sense of touch.

Sheets of sandpaper of eight different grades are purchased from very fine up to very coarse. Sheets are cut into pieces measuring approximately 5 ins. by 2 ins. and made up into sets containing one piece of each grade at the rate of two sets per Patrol. Each piece of sandpaper in each set is numbered on the back from one for the finest up to eight for the coarsest.

It is best if there can be one leader per Patrol but if necessary the activity can be supervised in each Patrol by Patrol Leaders who move round the hall one place.

Each member of the Patrol is blindfolded and comes forward in turn to where a set of the sandpapers is laid out in a line in mixed up order in front of him on a bench. The leader calls a particular number and the Scout by feel picks out that grade. A time limit of one minute is appropriate.

Two points are given each time the correct grade is found with half a point off down to nil for each grade in error, that is a Scout can make four attempts each turn. The Patrol can thus get maximum points of twice the number in the Patrol. To allow for different numbers in Patrols the actual points gained are worked out as a percentage of the possible maximum.

In order to get greater participation a second competition should be run simultaneously in each Patrol using the second set of sandpapers. In this case each Scout, again in turn, blindfolded, is handed the mixed up set of sandpapers and told to put them into correct order. Scoring in this case is by giving a maximum of 10 points with 1 point then being deducted for every mistake made. Average scores by members of each Patrol are worked out in this second competition.

109. Newspaper Information **NCM**

Each Patrol is supplied with a copy of the same issue of the same newspaper. The paper should be one which has sufficient sheets to enable at least one to be issued to all Scouts in the Patrol.

The leader prepares beforehand a list of questions to which the answer is found somewhere in the paper. For example he might call out "What happened to William B. Smith?" To which the answer might be, he broke his leg and the Patrol which first calls out this information is the winner and gains a point. Care must be taken that the answer is not hidden away in the fine print and too difficult to find. If the answer is not found within a reasonable time a clue can be given by announcing the number of the page on which the answer is to be found. Time limits can be made when necessary by announcing that there are 15 seconds to go. Questions should be selected so that there is at least one on each sheet.

110. Newspaper Words **NCM**

This is done in a rather similar way to Newspaper Information but in this case an actual word is called out and when this word is found a piece of paper with the word is torn out and brought to an umpire. Another difference in this game is that each turn can be continued in order to give a second and third place.

111. True or False **ALV**

The formation for this game and the one which follows is similar to that for the more active games of Baton Ball (No. 26) and Sack Tug (No. 27).

Patrols on one side of the room many conveniently play those on the other side. Each side forms a line graded by size from one end to the other and sit facing inwards along the length of the room but in contrast to Baton Ball taller and shorter Scouts face each other across the width and the numbering of Scouts in each line is done so that No. 1 is opposite No. 1.

At the end of the hall two chairs marked true are placed on each side of the centre facing down the length and chairs marked false are placed just beside the true chairs.

A statement is called out which may either be true or false followed by a number. The winner is the player who first sits on the correct chair on his side of the hall. It is not permitted to change chairs and if neither players sits on his correct chair no point is gained. Encouragement should be given for correctness as against mere speed. The first player on the correct chair is awarded two points while the other player receives one point if he has sat on the correct chair. Points gained can be used to determine individual Patrol as well as overall side results as in Baton Ball.

To a large extent the success of the game is determined by the interestingness of the statements given. It is not usually satisfactory to attempt to think up statements during the course of play. The game can be used to test and supply knowledge on the history of

Scouting, on Scouting subjects of all kinds and on past and future Troop activities with some non-Scouting items also thrown in. The statement will of course be confirmed if true and if untrue the correct information will be given. In either case the person running the game may sometimes usefully take the opportunity to expand very briefly on the subject of the statement. Numbers should occasionally be repeated in order to maintain alertness.

A good variation of this game giving a greater degree of participation is for it to be played from Patrol corners. Patrols are seated round the perimeter of the room facing inward with individual members numbered from one starting with the Patrol Leader up to whatever is the number of the most junior Scout in the largest Patrol, younger Scouts having two numbers if necessary. Out in the centre of the room in front of each Patrol are chalked true and false boxes.

A statement is called out followed by a number and all those with that number go out and stand in the true or false box. It is not practicable to assess who is first but there is a time limit of six seconds and a point is awarded to every Patrol whose Scout is standing in the correct box within the time. No player may change boxes.

112. Animal, Vegetable or Mineral **ALV**

This game is played in the same way as True or False except that instead of two chairs, three chairs are positioned for each side marked animal, vegetable and mineral. Materials are called out which can be categorised under one of the headings and the players of the number called endeavour to be first to sit on the correct chair.

Also as for True or False the game can be played from Patrol corners with three boxes chalked out in front of each Patrol. Care must be taken to make up an interesting list of materials and to exclude items on which there might be debate as for example coal or oil. The following are some suggestions:

> silk (A), salt (M), paper (V), lard (A), cricket ball (A), linseed oil (V), glass (m), kilt (A), granite (M), cotton (V), butter (A).

113. Object Bringing **ALV**

This game requires quick action among Patrol members operating from Patrol corners. Depending on objects asked to be brought the game can be run on a slightly frivolous note, as a fairly serious test of Scouting knowledge or as a mixture of both. It may be desired to have some staves and knotting ropes available.

A leader calls out objects which are to be brought to him. Two points are awarded to the Patrol bringing the object first and one point to the Patrol which is second. It should be made clear that no one may join a queue for assessment until a task called for is complete. The leader must move about so as to be nearest to different Patrols. The following are possible objects (or persons) to be called for:

Two shoes tied together with a reef knot.
A round turn and to half hitches on the left leg of a Scout
A Scout wearing two shirts
A coin with the date exactly divisable by 11
A piece of white cloth
A Scout stave with three correctly tied clove hitches
A Scout with left gymshoe on right foot and right gymshoe on left foot properly laced up
Three Scouts brought together at the waist with a packer knot.

114. Passing Round Activities **NCM**

All the activities described in Chapter XI on identifications using the passing round method are suitable for inclusion in a programme where a quiet competition is wanted involving knowledge of a particular subject.

CHAPTER XI

IDENTIFICATION COMPETITIONS BY PASSING ROUND METHOD

The passing round method provides means by which a large number of interesting activities of an identification nature can be carried out with all Scouts in the Troop being more or less continuously involved. The first of these identification activities is described in some detail with the intention that the general method will become apparent and can readily be applied to the other activities listed in this section.

Some of the identifications consist of series of cards which have been accumulated over the years from various sources including jumble sales and which may not always be generally available but they are given as ideas as to what can be found. Certainly once obtained, sets should be carefully preserved for bringing out again in years ahead.

It should be found fully acceptable to have at least four of these identification activities of one kind or another using the passing round method during a Scout year.

115. Contents of Bags — NCM

Materials and objects are placed in cloth bags and have to be identified by touch.

Bags must be made of material which is strong, opaque and non-porous but also soft enough to allow the contents to be easily felt. It is not in fact necessary to have bags as such. Very suitable are pieces of cloth about 15 ins. square which are gathered up round the items to be identified and tied up tightly with twine. Old tent material may be available and suitable. Each bag must be numbered either directly on to the cloth or by tie on label.

If there are only six Scouts in the Troop then the activity is easily organised. Six bags only are necessary. The Scouts sit equally spaced round the circumference of a circle about 12 ft. in diameter. Each has a pencil and a piece of paper with the numbers one to six down one side. The bags are distributed one to each Scout and a minute allowed to identify and write down the contents. The bags are then passed round the circle one place clockwise until everyone has received them all. The answers can be self-marked there and then as a leader holds up each bag in turn and invites suggestions as to the contents.

A similar routine can be followed for up to 12 Scouts using a larger circle and 12 bags and sheets of paper with numbers 1 to 12. As more than one Patrol will be involved a refinement of the marking will be to work out Patrol average marks for Patrol competition purposes.

It should be noted that it is not necessary for the number of Scouts to equal the number of bags. If, for example, there are nine Scouts and 12 bags then a spare chair is inserted in the circle on which three spare bags are placed in a row tangential to the circle and at each change the movement on the chair is continued clockwise with one bag being taken from one end of the row and one bag being added at the other end. There is indeed no reason why this arrangement should not be used for six Scouts to receive 12 bags if an activity on that scale is desired.

When the number of Scouts is in excess of 12 and certainly when in excess of about 18 it may become difficult to provide that number of different bags and in any case the activity will go on too long if every Scout is examining every bag. Alternatively if one gives only one bag to a Patrol of six Scouts it will almost certainly be monopolised by one or two senior members with consequent negligible participation by younger Scouts. The following method is recommended for six Patrols with adaptations as described for Patrols down to three.

The critical number of bags to have is 18 and this it should be emphasised is also the number of items to be used in the other identification activities referred to hereafter. However, if in any activity it is inordinately difficult to get 18 completely different subjects for identification then it is acceptable to duplicate one or two provided the numbering is so arranged that the duplicates go to different Patrol sections. In such circumstances it is reasonable to announce that there may be duplicates.

Given below is a list of 20 items which may be helpful in forming a set of 18 for contents of bags identification.

Steel wool	India rubber
Paper clips	Coffee
Three 5p pieces	Remembrance Day Poppy
Three 2p pieces	Buttons
Woggle	Torch battery
Rice	Acorns
Lentils	Monkey nuts
Dried peas	Milk bottle tops
Tea	Wood screws
Golf tee	Washers

After numbering from 1 to 18 the bags are sorted into three groups of 1–6, 7–12 and 13–18. It is desirable to have variations between groups in that for example similar materials such as coffee, tea, lentils, rice and dried peas should not all be in the same group. Six sets of three bags are then formed by taking one bag from each group and the sets kept separate in plastic or paper bags for distribution to Patrols. If, as in numbers of activities noted later on, the identification series consists of cards then each set of three cards is kept together by a paper clip.

Each Patrol is issued with three pieces of paper (A4 divided into three across the length) held together by a paper clip. Each piece has a space for the Patrol name at the top and on the first down the side are numbers 1–6, on the second numbers 7–12 and on the third numbers 13–18. It will be useful to have a store of pieces of paper headed up and numbered in this way probably reproduced by photocopying. The Patrol Leader divides his Patrol into three sections, each generally consisting of two Scouts, and gives one of the pieces of the paper to each section.

A set of three bags is given to each Patrol and each section immediately takes the bag in the 1–6, 7–12 or 13–18 group as on its numbered paper. One and a half minutes are allowed for sections to identify the contents of their bag and write down the answer opposite the number on the piece of paper. It is not sacrosanct that sections attempt to identify only their own bag and consultation can take place throughout the Patrol but each section is finally responsible for writing down the contents. In any case the time has been deliberately kept short so that it will hardly be possible for a Patrol expert to do the whole lot.

On the expiry of one and a half minutes each Patrol passes on its three bags to the next Patrol clockwise round the room. This requires a routine if bags are not to be mixed up. A warning instruction "prepare to change" is first given when Patrols gather their three bags together and this is followed by "change" when one Scout from each Patrol delivers the bags to the next Patrol. Allowing half a minute for the actual handover, changes continue approximately every two minutes until all Patrols have received all the bags. Bags and answer sheets are then collected in. A numbered answer sheet should be available for marking. Half points may sometimes be appropriate in instances for example such as scourer for steel wool.

If there are less than six Patrols then sets of three bags are located at blank stances which can conveniently be together at one end of the hall. To avoid bags getting out of their sets of three a leader should look after the blank stances. For example, if there are only three Patrols he will have three sets of three bags and at the time of change he will move these clockwise passing, facing inwards, one set on to the Patrol on his left and receiving one set from the Patrol on his right. In such circumstances it is not enough to have only nine bags as the activity would then be thought to be inadequate in length.

116. Picture Cards **NCMV**

Frederick Warne and Company have published a series of sets of picture cards of which the following are especially suitable for identification activities.

British Birds
Wild Flowers
British Wild Animals
Trees
Flags

All the sets consist of 32 cards each of which has a picture on one side and descriptive text on the other. The excess over 18 allows a selection to be made and more difficult identifications to be left out. After numbering the cards and listing the answers the names on the picture side are blacked or white opaqued out. The text is left in on the back of the cards as aiding identification except that the name itself is blotted out wherever it occurs. The cards are sorted into lots of three and the activity proceeds as described for Contents of Bags.

If it is thought that any of the sets of cards are too difficult then they can be made easier by issuing an unnumbered list of say the 18 trees so reducing the activity to matching 18 pictures with 18 names. A list is needed for each section of each Patrol amounting to 18 copies if there are six Patrols. The activity can be repeated in four or five months time without issue of a list.

Difficulty may be experienced nowadays in obtaining the Frederick Warne picture cards but at not much greater expense sets can be readily made by cutting pictures from cheaper pocket books of birds, flowers, animals and trees and mounting them on card. Particularly to be mentioned for this purpose are books in the Frederick Warne Observer and Blandford Mini-Guide series. National flags commonly appear in advertisements and are also available in the form of a gummed sheet.

Other sets of picture cards known to be available are:

Mistake Cards
What Object Cards

The Mistake Cards include such items as a bus entrance being on the offside and traffic lights being in the wrong order while the What Object Cards include photographs of a lemon squeezer side on and a light bulb from above.

One should be constantly on the look out for material which can be made into a series of picture cards for an identification activity using the passing round method.

117. Dimensions **NCM**

Consideration is given to estimation of dimensions as an instructional activity in No. 54 and one competition suitable to follow this is the estimation of dimensions of objects using the passing round method.

18 objects are numbered and divided into six lots of three. Labelling must make clear what dimension is required. Part of the success of the activity obtains from providing interesting objects to be estimated. These can include quite short lengths such as coins (an old penny for example) of only an inch or two up to a wooden bench of around 8 ft. and a length of rope of 20 ft. Another object being passed round might be a climbing rope which must not be undone. It is also a good idea for one or two of the estimations to consist of a piece of paper on which is an instruction such as estimate the width of the hall or the maximum internal height.

It must be made clear that it is not permissible to use any form of ruler for direct measurement and for this purpose a Scout stave ringed in feet and inches is a ruler but the use of personal measurements is to be encouraged.

A quite high degree of accuracy can be obtained for some objects. It is important that the answers be precisely known and a mathematically inclined leader equipped with a calculating machine will mark the results based on percentage error above or below actuals. A simpler method of marking is to give 3, 2 or 1 points for the three answers nearest to the true measurement.

118. Weights **NCM**

Reference should be made to weight estimation as an instructional activity in No. 55.

18 numbered objects are passed round for estimation of weight and the whole activity is carried out very similarly to the estimation of dimensions. Again the objects should in themselves be interesting and can in particular include items of camp equipment ranging from a small aluminium dixie up to the heaviest Patrol tent.

It may also be possible to include one or two items such as a heavy piece of furniture which is not passed round but which the Scouts go to on receipt of instructions on a numbered piece of paper. The weights of heavy objects can be determined by using bathroom scales or a large spring balance.

119. Numbers **NCM**

A passing round competition based on numbers can provide a good follow up to an instructional session on the subject to which reference is made in No. 56.

In this instance it is difficult to get 18 items which are completely different in nature. However, the important thing is that each Patrol section should receive items which are dissimilar and this can readily be done. Given below are 18 suggested items for numbers estimation.

Nails in screw top jar.

Dried peas in screw top jar.

Pine cones or gravel stones in screw top jar.

The number of dots on three pieces of white card of A4 size having approximately 100, 200 and 400 black dots.

The total length in inches of a number of uncrossing lines drawn on three pieces of white card of A4 size. These might consist of around 20 lines totalling about 40 ins., 30 lines totalling about 60 ins. and 40 lines totalling about 80 ins.

The sum total of numbers ranging from one to nine written on three pieces of white card of A4 size. These could consist of around 30 numbers totalling about 150, 40 numbers totalling about 200 and 50 numbers totalling about 250.

Numbers of words on three sheets of print mounted on card.

Number of entries in a page of telephone directory mounted on card though if need be this could be increased to three.

A piece of card on which it is stated that a number estimate is to be made of some particular feature of the Troop meeting room. This could be the number of vertical lining boards on the walls or the number of ceiling tiles.

The number of Scout staves in a closely packed pile of about 40 Scout staves which must not be touched.

Each item must be clearly numbered and it is most important that it be carefully stated on each item just what is to be estimated.

The items should be arranged into lots of three so that similar items do not arrive at Patrols at the same time. Large bags will be necessary to keep lots of three together for initial distribution to Patrols. Two minutes, rather than 1½ minutes, is a better time for having each item in this activity. Passing on must be vigorously enforced and it is helpful to give a 15 second warning of time up.

The answers must be carefully preserved and can often best be obtained by counting during the actual process of compiling the item. Considerable inaccuracy can be expected in the answers for some items and the marking scheme must cater for a wide variation above and below the true figure. People will be interested to know the answers and these should be put up on a noticeboard.

The activity can be used every two or three years and much time can be saved in the future by carefully storing away all the materials.

120. Tree Twigs Passing Round NCMV

Passing round twigs for identification provides a useful follow up competition to a tree identification instruction session as described in No. 45.

Twig specimens are collected from 18 different common trees or for a lesser number with duplicates, as covered in the instruction session and numbered using tie on labels. In splitting down the twigs into groups care should be taken that there is variation and that each Patrol section receives at least one twig from a coniferous tree and one from a paired bud broadleaved tree such as ash or sycamore. Plastic carrier bags are very helpful for quick and correct initial distribution of lots of three to Patrols. The competition can be done at two distinct times of the year with trees in bud or in leaf although evergreen trees, including most conifers, will have the same general appearance throughout the year. If 18 different twigs are not available then there is no reason why some should not be included twice taking care that the duplicates go to different Patrol sections.

121. Paint Colours NCM

Paint manufacturers tend to give their paints names such as cornflower, jasmine or spice which are descriptive of the colours but which a person would not necessarily use for say mid-blue, light yellow or dark brown.

18 colours are cut out from a paint manufacturer's colour chart and mounted without names on numbered cards. The cards are then put into lots of three for passing round Patrols for name identification. Since it is unreasonable that a person would invent a name such as cornflower for a particular shade of blue it is necessary for each section of each Patrol to have a list, in no particular order, of the 18 colours selected from the colour chart, that is 18 lists will be required if there are six Patrols. In shades of blue for example the essence of the activity might be to distinguish between pinefrost, summer blue, harebell and cornflower.

122. Object Passing Round **NCM**

18 objects of a kind about which questions can be asked afterwards are got together and put into lots of three for passing round. They are not numbered.

The activity can be an opportunity to let the Troop see items of historical interest and might include one or two old photographs, a pennant which the Troop won, an old Coffee Morning ticket and an antler found on a hike. There might be one or two modern Troop photographs, nature objects or pictures and miscellaneous items such as a book, a knot, a cardboard box, a map, a piece of wood, an old badge and a dish cloth.

Patrols are split into three sections and each section receives an object to inspect but it does not matter which object.

When Patrols have seen all the items they are collected in and each Patrol receives a sheet of paper on which to write down the answers to questions about the objects. The questions are called out for all to hear by a leader and for example might be name three people in a particular photograph, what is the length of the piece of wood, what two words are on the badge and how many points has the antler. The Patrol Leader will probably have the sheet of paper and write down the question number and the answer but as not everyone in the Patrol will have been able to examine fully all the items the activity will have to be a collective effort with information being fed to the Patrol Leader by individuals who have knowledge of particular items.

It is not necessary to have a question on every object and about 12 questions in all will probably be sufficient.

CHAPTER XII

RELAY FORMATION GAMES

The value of relay games in Scouting has in the past probably been somewhat over-rated. Usually they give little opportunity for the Patrol to function as a team since the result is determined by the automatic summation of individual performances while the Patrol Leader's leadership contribution can be little more than one of exhortation. Further the form of the activity is such that it can highlight an individual's inadequacies resulting perhaps in loss of self-confidence and in unpopularity in the Patrol.

There are some relays however which are enjoyed because they have an element of attractive novelty and there are others which are useful because they give practice in some particular technique. There are also included in this section some games which are not really true relays but for which it is convenient that Patrols take up relay formation.

By relay formation is meant that Patrols are in single file, normally with the Patrol Leader in the front spread over the width of the hall behind a line drawn across the hall about 10 ft. from one end. In instances where a relay requires particular knowledge, ability in a technique or special preparation then only a cross reference is given in this section and a description of the relay will be found as a follow up activity to an instructional session in the subject.

Some relays which may be quite well known, are omitted on the grounds that they are not thought particularly inspiring.

Patrols should be equalised by designating Scouts of average ability in smaller Patrols to run twice to make up to the number in the largest Patrol. In cases of serious discrepancy Patrols may be combined with each of the combined Patrols getting the same points.

After making his run in whatever form it may be Scouts go to the back of the Patrol though this may not apply in some games which are not true relays and for which the formation is only assumed for convenience.

There are several relay formation games which involve carrying members of the Patrol. It can sometimes happen that a member of a Patrol is too heavy to be reasonably carried by the others. In such circumstances a useful rule to make is that all Patrols can, at their choice, omit carrying one particular person but there must be a second carry of any other person in substitute.

123. Bench Relay **ARY**

Each Patrol takes with them into relay formation two seating benches. If the benches are not all identical then if possible Patrols should have similar two benches, for example, a long bench and a shorter bench. Unequal numbers in Patrols does not matter unless extreme.

All Scouts and the two benches are completely behind the starting line. On the start whistle all Scouts in the Patrol are to touch the far end of the hall and to return behind the starting line without touching the floor using the benches as large moving stepping stones.

If any Scout touches the floor the Patrol must remain stationary for ten seconds under the timing of an umpire. Benches must be completely back across the starting line. The game takes only a few minutes and all Patrols should be placed.

Another form of this game called Bench Pursuit and requiring a total of only four benches is described in No. 40.

124. Staggers Relay **ARY**

A cross is chalked on the floor opposite each Patrol about 8 ft. from the far end of the hall. Each Patrol has a pole about 33 ins. long such as a broken broom stick or Scout stave.

On the start whistle the first member of each Patrol runs with the pole to the chalk cross. He places one end of the pole on the cross and holding the pole vertically places both hands, one on top of the other, and then his forehead on the top of the pole. He then makes six complete revolutions clockwise and runs back holding the pole to set off the second member of the Patrol.

The reason for the title of the relay will readily become apparent. Leaders should be available to see that Scouts do not hurt themselves by running against the side walls and also to be near the turning where the problem may be Scouts losing count and making too many revolutions rather than too few.

125. Stepping Stone Relay **ARY**

The relay is conveniently played with the wooden blocks measuring

10 ins. x 6 ins. x 4 ins. as used for the game Logger (see No. 35). Two blocks are required per Patrol.

A line is drawn across the hall about 15 ft. in advance of Patrols standing in relay formation. Using the blocks as movable stepping stones Scouts have to get across the line without touching the floor. On crossing the line each Scout returns carrying the blocks to set off the next member of the Patrol.

In any instance of touching the floor while using the stepping stones the Scout is required to remain stationary for the period of a slow count of five by an umpire.

126. Tenniquoit Relay **ALY**

The game requires ability to throw a tenniquoit ring accurately and to catch it on a Scout stave at a range of about 15 ft. The actual relay is best preceeded by a period of practice in Patrol corners under Patrol Leader supervision. Ideally there should be two tenniquoit rings per Patrol to allow practice in two groups of three.

A line is drawn across the hall about 15 ft. in advance of Patrols standing in relay formation. No. 1 stands on the line holding a tenniquoit ring and on the order of go throws the ring to be caught on a Scout stave held by No. 2. No. 3 functions as fielder and returns the ring to No. 1 if it does not go on to the stave. When No. 2 catches the ring he passes the stave to No. 3, takes the ring to the line and commences throwing to No. 3. No. 1 goes to the back of the Patrol and No. 4 takes up the position of fielder. The relay ends when No. 1 comes to the front and catches the ring unless extra turns are necessary to equalise Patrols.

An advantage of this relay is that three persons are simultaneously occupied.

127. Numbers Relay **ARMY**

100 small squares are drawn up on a sheet of paper in a square block with 10 small square sides. A suitable size fitting conveniently on A4 paper is small squares of 17 mm. sides giving a large square of 17 cm. side.

In a completely random manner the numbers 1 to 100 are written into the small squares and the sheet then reproduced either by photocopying or by use of ball point pen and carbon papers so that there is one identical sheet per Patrol.

The sheets are placed on chairs or benches in a line about 6 ft. out from the opposite end of the hall from the Patrols standing in relay formation.

On the start whistle the first member of each Patrol runs out to his sheet and looks for No. 1. When he has found it he indicates it to an umpire by putting his finger on the square. He then looks for No. 2 and if he finds it similarly indicates it to the umpire. Approximately every 20 seconds the whistle is blown and the next player runs out. The player at the sheet tells the next player the number being looked for and then immediately returns to the end of the Patrol. The game continues for about four minutes and the Patrol which has reached the highest number is the winner.

An umpire can reasonably look after two Patrols. If there is a serious shortage of leaders to act as umpires then the matter can be got over by the Patrol Leaders functioning as umpires by moving to other Patrols.

128. Hammer and Nails Relay **ALMY**

The purpose of the relay is to test the ability to knock in nails quickly and without bending.

A line of benches is put out across the hall about 8 ft. out from the other end to where the Patrols are standing in relay formation.

On the benches opposite each Patrol is placed a hammer, a block of wood approximately 4 ins. square and 2 ins. thick and a supply of 1½ in. nails in a saucer.

On the blowing of the whistle Patrol Leaders run out and begin hammering nails into one face of the block of wood. The whistle is blown after about 25 seconds and the next member of the Patrol runs out and takes over from the Patrol Leader who immediately returns to the end of the Patrol

Successive members of the Patrol come out roughly every 25 seconds as the whistle is blown. The game continues for about three minutes when the final whistle is blown. A count is then carefully made with each nail correctly knocked in counting one and each nail which is in a bent over state counting minus two. A second session can be held using another face of the block.

It is important to use soft wood blocks as knocking nails into a hard wood such as oak will be found too difficult. 60 nails per Patrol should be sufficient for two sessions. It is preferable that the hammers be all of the same design and the activity merits the purchase if necessary and the storing away for the future, of cheaper fairly lightweight hammers to the number of one per Patrol. In the interests of safety the changeover should be at the wood blocks with nobody running holding a hammer.

129. Highland Games **ARMY**

The following six items are made available for Highland Games.

Shot —Inflated round balloon.
Discus —piece of light card about 1½ ins. square.
Hammer —match.
Javelin —drinking straw.
Cricket ball —piece of aluminium foil ½in. square tightly compressed.
Caber —inflated long balloon.

Each Patrol receives a set of the miniaturised equipment for about five minutes practice and for decision as to which Scouts are going to do which events. All Scouts must do at least one event with more than one occurring only if there are less than six Scouts in the Patrol. If numbers are around five per Patrol then the caber can be omitted. If numbers in the Patrol exceed the number of events then two Scouts do one event but with only the best result counting for points purposes.

As each event is called a Scout quickly comes forward from each Patrol and stands on a relay position line drawn across the hall near one end. Each Scout throws in succession on call of Patrol name. Judges quickly come out from the side to mark the distance achieved with a chalk line and Patrol initial. The distance is the rearmost part of the object as it has come to rest though point of landing may be necessary for balloons if they are blown by draughts.

Time may allow a second throw but only the best throw counts and no Patrol can gain more than one place in an event. It is suggested that 3, 2 or 1 points be given to the first, second and third in each event. Damp cloths are need to remove chalk marks between events.

A valuable part of the activity is the practice and selection. During the contest everyone should be seated so they have a reasonable view and so that they can quickly come forward for their event. There should be a good reserve of equipment to replace items which become damaged or lost especially in the practice period. It is not essential that items be projected in the traditional manner.

130. Progressive Leap **ARY**

The objective of this competition is to get a member of the Patrol as far as possible in advance of the relay base line following a succession of standing jumps by all Scouts in the Patrol.

The first member of the Patrol stands just behind the base line and on the order to jump leaps forward as far as he can. There must be absolutely no movement of feet after landing however wide apart they may be. The second members of Patrols then come out and place their toes immediately behind the heels of the Scouts who have jumped first. The first jumpers then go to the back of the Patrol and the second members make a standing jump forward. The process continues until all Scouts have jumped with second jump being made by designated Scouts of average ability where necessary to make up to the number in the largest Patrol.

Some umpiring may be required on account of occasional over-balancing on landing. Also because it is of interest to see how Patrols are progressing after each leap, it is best if the jumping is synchronised. This is done by the leader running the activity giving each time the instruction "prepare to leap" followed two seconds later by the order "leap".

In the event of the hall being of insufficient length to accommodate the combined jumps (each jump will probably average about 5 ft.) then the jumping must be done in two parts. The end of the first part is marked to the furthest toe line with chalk when the end wall comes within range. A second part then starts from the base line and the two distances are added together.

131. Stretcher Relay **ALY**
See No. 74.

132. Four Handed Seat Relay **ALY**
See No. 44.

133. Pharaoh's Chariot Relay **ALY**
See No. 71.

134. Tree Identification Relay **ALMYV**
See No. 45

135. Rescue Line Relay **ALY**
See No. 57.

136. Stilts Relay **ALMY**
See No. 73.

137. Street Knowledge Relay **ALMY**
See No. 48.

CHAPTER XIII

CIRCUIT ACTIVITIES

There are numbers of excellent games, competitions and instructional activities which because of limitations on equipment, on space available, in the number of people who can do it simultaneously or because there is a need for detailed instruction in small numbers by a specialist cannot be undertaken by the Troop all at the same time unless numbers do not exceed two Patrols. Activities in these circumstances can however often be put over very satisfactorily by means of a circuit Troop meeting.

In the circuit type meeting a Troop of six Patrols is split into three sections each normally consisting of two Patrols. If Patrols are not of equal size it may be possible to combine them in such a way that three sections are roughly the same.

If a two hour Troop meeting is assumed of which 45 minutes is taken up with opening and closing procedures and perhaps beginning and end games then we are left with 75 minutes during which each section can devote 25 minutes to three different activities. What these may be does of course to some extent depend on the meeting facilities available. Perhaps there may be a hall, a leaders' room, a kitchen (not necessarily to be used only for a cooking activity) or separate classrooms, or it may be suitable for some activities to use either end of the main meeting hall though ideally it is best if Scouts are not aware of the item to which they are next proceeding. Sometimes an item can be done outside the Headquarters and on occasion more than one item may be done during the 25 minute stay at a base.

Some of the items may be technical requiring knowledgeable instructors but there is no reason why one position on the circuit should not be taken up with a competition or some game of a purely recreational nature but with the opportunity being taken to do something which is only convenient for small numbers. An advantage of the circuit type Troop meeting is that it can provide worthwhile occupation for Instructors and for Venture Scouts functioning as Assistant Leaders. The Scout Leader should try and avoid being tied down himself at one base and be available to indicate time to change round after giving prior warning four minutes in advance.

Patrol points will be given for competitions and games and possibly also for standard acquired in instructional activities.

Circuit activities can be especially useful in getting Scouts going on the gaining of particular badges.

It is worth noting that provided there are two Patrols in a section almost any game or activity can be done as part of a circuit. There are however some activities which due to requirements of equipment or instruction can only be done in a circuit. It is items in this category which are covered in detail below. Sometimes it may be desired to provide a circuit in order to cover one particularly important subject such as, for example, mouth to mouth ventilation and it is not essential that the games or activities at the other bases be "circuit only" items.

Circuit type meetings should not be held too often. Numbers of the activities given below will also lend themselves very well to being done as part of circuit at an indoor based winter weekend where time may not be at such a sharp premium.

138. Roller Bandaging **NLTM**

It could reasonably be held that it is not justified to purchase enough lint and bandages of various sizes to enable a Troop of 36 Scouts all to practise roller bandaging simultaneously and in any case it is unlikely that sufficient people will be available to give the necessary detailed instruction.

One or two Patrols is an ideal number to instruct in roller bandaging and the subject is therefore very suitable to be included in a circuit programme.

Description is given in some Scout books but more detail will probably be wanted as given in numbers of first aid books.

139. Mouth-to-Mouth Ventilation **NLTM**

In all except the smallest of Troops some form of circuit type programme will be required to put over mouth-to-mouth ventilation satisfactorily.

The subject is so important that a large Scout group will be justified in possessing a practice manikin of its own. A manikin may be available at Scout County/Area or District level or the local Red Cross may be able to supply one quite possibly also with an instructor.

It is to be noted that the whole of the session does not have to be done as part of the circuit. There is no reason why an initial ten minute exposition and demonstration should not be given to the whole Troop together. It would however, be a matter for intolerable delay if say all 36 Scouts had to sit waiting for their turn to practise. The Troop therefore goes straight into a three section circuit programme of which one item is mouth-to-mouth ventilation with the manikin.

It might be held that even with only 12 Scouts there is still too much time wasting and there could be further split down so that during the 25 minute period half the time is spent doing mouth-to-mouth ventilation and half the time doing a puzzle type item as perhaps selected from Chapter X or from No. 197.

Mouth-to-mouth ventilation is covered in 'Challenge and Adventure'.

140. Recovery Position **NLT**

This important first aid procedure is described in Scout and first aid literature. It is a subject in which individual personal practice and instruction is required and is therefore very suitable to be covered in a circuit.

Comparison can be made with the arrangement for learning mouth-to-mouth ventilation (No. 139) where time, and repetition by the instructor, can be saved by having the initial instruction and demonstration before the commencement of the circuit with personal practice being done at one of the circuit points.

141. Holger-Neilsen Resuscitation **NLT**

This method of resuscitation is described in first aid books. The reasons for including instruction in the Holger-Neilsen method as part of a circuit are the same as for instruction in the recovery position and the same arrangement can be made as described for No. 140 immediately above.

142. Rope Stretcher **ALT**

A description of the making of a rope stretcher appeared in the Advanced Scout Standard book. A piece of light rope at least 50 ft. long is required for each stretcher and if the Troop has 12 of these it will usually be possible for all members in two Patrols to make one each. Or the Scouts can operate in pairs if space, or number of ropes, is a limiting factor.

It should be remembered that a rope stretcher is intended to be used with a large number of bearers and the Scouts will have to get together to try out their stretchers with a patient.

143. Line Coiling and Throwing **ALT**

In throwing a line, in mountaineering and in putting rope away after pioneering there is great need to be able to coil rope efficiently.

In this session we are particularly concerned with the ability to coil and throw a light rope quickly and accurately for life-saving purposes. It is assumed that the victim is about 30 ft. away either off the end of a pier in water or in a hole in ice. The need is to tie with great speed in the end of the rope a bowline of sufficient size to go over the shoulders and to coil and throw the rope with accuracy.

It has been suggested that the Troop possess 50 ft. lengths of light rope at the rate of two per Patrol and this should provide one rope each for everyone in the session. The quick tying of the bowline may be difficult for some people but the life or death importance of the subject will, it is hoped, encourage the attainment of proficiency. The size is measured from the rope in the hands with arms stretched apart.

The coiling of the rope requires a method to prevent twisting. In this case the bowline knot is first placed on the upturned right palm with the loop hanging downwards. The left hand is taken down the rope to maximum extension. The left hand then carries the rope to the outside of the right hand and lays the rope across the right palm from outside to inside so forming a clockwise loop hanging below the right hand. Further loops are formed in a similar way until sufficient have been accumulated to provide a convenient throwing weight. Care is taken that the remainder of the rope lying on the floor (pier) will run free and the thrower make sure the end of the rope is carefully secured to some object, given to a bystander or securely held underfoot before each throw.

Accuracy of throwing is tested by having another Scout in position to receive the bowline. In the event of failure the rope is quickly pulled in with both hands to lie at the feet and then recoiled into the right hand for a second throw. It is a good standard to be able to make a bowline, coil the rope and make a first throw in 30 seconds.

It will be important to advise the Scouts that there could be circumstances where other and more rapid rescue action than rope throwing as being practised would be appropriate.

144. Kim's Game Change **NCT**

Approximately 24 objects are laid out on a table roughly 4 ft. square. The objects should be large and small and to some extent have an interest in themselves.

The Patrol is told that changes are going to be made. They are then allowed to look at the objects for one minute after which they leave the room. The leader then makes 12 alterations to the layout. Examples are removing objects altogether, adding new ones, altering the position of objects, turning objects round, opening a book at a different page, turning over an ice axe, replacing a blue headed match with a red headed one.

When the changes have been made the Patrol returns and has eight minutes to state verbally the 12 changes. On the grounds that the changes might all be eventually guessed and in order to discourage a frivolous approach the number of statements of change which can be made is restricted to 18. It is quite in order for the Patrol to discuss possible changes among themselves.

It is very necessary for the person running the activity to have a list of the changes so that he can tick off the correct answers as they are given and also restore the layout to the original position for the next Patrol.

There should be no difficulty in fitting in two Patrols during the 25 minute period but an additional activity will be needed for Patrols while they are not doing the Kim's Game. Very suitable is finding the differences in a set of similar pictures (No. 96) or one of the quizzes from the Handbook of Indoor Games and Contests (No. 197). There is the advantage that no leader supervision is required for these secondary activities.

145. Belay System **ALTM**

A knowledgeable person talks briefly on the place of the belay system in mountaineering. Information is contained in various mountaineering manuals.

The procedure can be demonstrated and carried out practically by attachment to hooks, wall bars or to other suitable projections. In order to emphasise that the subject is one very much for real it is essential that at least one proper climbing rope be on hand but practice can be done in pairs using 50 ft. lengths of knotting rope.

An important part of the session is that everyone should be able to tie a bowline quickly, securely and tightly around his waist. A considerable amount of instructional effort will probably have to be devoted to this particular aspect and a supplementary instructor, well warned so that he can be sure he can do it, is likely to be very useful.

146. Abseiling **ALTM**

In some Scout Headquarters there may be a vertical door high up in a wall giving access to a loft. This may allow the demonstration of abseiling procedure and the carrying out of short abseils.

A competent person must be available to supervise this activity and assistants will be required. Method using karabiner is advised.

It is possible to demonstrate the taking up of position at floor level using hooks or other attachments on the wall and several sets of rope, slings and karabiner will be required.

This session of instruction should be looked upon as preparation for abseiling down a significant face and there is probably little point in having the activity at the Headquarters if there is not much prospect of doing the real thing.

147. Paraffin Pressure Stoves and Lamps **NLTM**

A knowledgeable person gives a short talk on the construction and method of operation of paraffin pressure stoves and lamps with particular reference to problems and faults which can arise. These are so varied and are learnt about with only such a depth of experience that even the most confident Scout who has already passed the test should not fail to benefit. It would be hoped that there would be at least one stove or lamp between two which they will light.

148. Knots and Lashings (Circuit) **NLT**

The learning of knots and lashings lends itself particularly to circuits where there is opportunity for instruction in small groups.

The excellent Pioneer badge has in its requirements ability to make the following knots and lashings: sheet-bend, clove hitch, round turn and two half hitches, bowline, timber hitch, sheepshank, square lashing, and sheer lashing.

At this session in the circuit as many as possible of these knots and lashings are taught. A good supply of 8 ft. knotting ropes will be required. To some extent the ground covered will depend on how much the Scouts already know but the main purpose of the session will be to stimulate interest and to encourage massive gaining of the badge.

The requirements of the badge will be gone over and a photocopy given out. It will for example be said that there will be opportunity to do the outdoor collective project at the next weekend camp and a date will be announced for the testing of the individual indoor sections of the badge.

Additional to the above the Advanced Pioneer badge requires the making of harvesters hitch, double sheetbend, fisherman's knot, rolling hitch, figure of eight lashing, diagonal lashing and sailmakers whipping all of which are very suitable for learning in circuit sessions.

149. Splicing **NLT**

It is pleasing that splicing again has a specific place in the badge scheme as a result of inclusion of the back and eye splices in the Chief Scout's Award and Advanced Pioneer badge and a 25 minute session in a circuit programme provides an ideal opportunity to teach a subject which many boys find intriguing.

Obviously the Troop must have someone who has ability in the subject but splicing is not really difficult and it is very well worthwhile for a leader to become familiar with the making of these two splices by study from a ropework text book.

A piece of lightweight three strand rope about 30 ins. long will be required for each Scout to enable him to make one splice in each end. Old guy ropes or otherwise defective rope may be available for this practice purpose but even if it is necessary to go out and buy new rope the cost is not severe. It will be helpful if photocopy sheets showing the stages in making the splices are available. Some boys like to puzzle these things out on their own and they should be allowed to take away the photocopy sheets and rope.

150. Stave Extrication **NCT**

The Troop's stock of Scout staves is gathered together up to a total of about 40 but with at least 20. The umpire holds all the staves together in a tight bundle standing on the floor vertically. He then allows the bundle to fall so that as many staves as possible lie on top of each other in a single pile.

The first person from one Patrol comes out and picks up the stave which he thinks he can do most readily without causing movement to any other stave. If there is no movement he keeps the stave. The first person of the other Patrol then makes an attempt and Patrols continue turn about with succeeding members until all staves have been recovered.

For the first one or two turns no more may be involved than picking up staves which have rolled clear of the pile but instances can soon occur where extremely difficult and intricate extrication is required. The slightest movement of another stave results in loss of turn.

Occasionally the umpire may adjust the pile to relieve an impossibly interlocked position. The winner is the Patrol having the best total from two or three sessions. It may be that 25 minutes will not be required for this game and in this case a convenient item to proceed to is Stave Bowls as given immediately below.

151. Stave Bowls **ART**

A circle is drawn 8 ft. in diameter with the nearest part of the circle about 15 ft. in front of a base line which is 12 ft. long and which extends 6 ft. on either side of the nearest point to the circle. There should be a clear space of about 6 ft. on the side of the circle remote from the base line.

Each Patrol takes eight staves which are divided as nearly as possible equally between their Scouts. The staves of one Patrol are distinguished by marking with chalk.

Each Patrol stands behind its 6 ft. section of base line and successive Scouts from each Patrol in turn slide their staves along the floor with the object of getting them into the circle or knocking out the staves of the other Patrol.

The staves of each Patrol completely in the circle are carefully counted after the end of each round. It is unlikely that 25 minutes will be required for this game and it is suggested that it is played with Stave Extrication as described immediately previously.

It is in fact quite possible to play Stave Bowls as part of an ordinary Troop meeting. Up to three Patrols can play together provided there are enough staves and they are adequately distinguished. Patrols need not have exactly the same number of Scouts but must be given exactly the same total number of staves. Where three Patrols are playing the number of staves per Patrol should not exceed six unless this is unavoidable because Patrols contain more than six members.

The base line should consist of the arc of a circle 18 ft. long drawn 15 ft. from the circle and marked into three 6 ft. sections. Order of bowling must be carefully observed. The game can be played in duplicate with either two or three Patrols at opposite ends of the hall.

152. Estimating Inaccessible Widths and Heights **NLT**

Various estimation activities which can be done by the Troop altogether are suggested elsewhere in this book but there are methods of estimating inaccessible widths and heights which require personal learning and practice and this can be conveniently done as a circuit item.

The width method as well as being in Scouting for Boys was given in a section on surveying in the Advanced Scout Standard book. Following demonstration the Scouts estimate widths chalked out on the floor. Scout staves or wooden one foot rules can be used to construct the diagram used for the estimation. A supply of chalk and also of wet cloths to rub out chalk marks will be required.

Scouts can work in pairs. They both estimate the same width from opposite sides and then measure the width to see who is nearer.

A method of estimating heights against a Scout stave is also described in Scouting for Boys and in the Advanced Scout Standard book. This can be used in the Troop room to measure particular heights. This method requires Scouts to work in pairs and each Scout in turn can make his own estimation.

Another method of estimating heights is to hold a pencil vertically in front of the face. The pencil is then moved nearer or further away until it exactly appears to cover the height which it is desired to measure. The pencil is then turned through 90 degrees to lie horizontal and the length covered by the pencil at the same distance from the observer is the height of the object which can now be conveniently measured on the flat. For example the height of a room in a corner can be transferred by this means to be measured along the foot of a wall.

Estimations by the two methods should be compared with each other and also with actual heights as may be obtainable by real measurement with Scout staves or measuring tapes.

Although it will not often be able to be actually done at a Troop meeting it is also worthwhile to give a description of estimating heights by the shadow method. This is based upon direct proportion. For example if a shadow 6 ft. long is cast by a Scout stave 4 ft. high, then if a shadow from a tree is 90 ft. long the tree will be 60 ft. high.

153. Balls into Circle NCT

This game has been classified as a circuit activity because 12 hollow plastic balls are required for each Patrol and that quantity may not be available where there are six Patrols.

Concentric circles are drawn on the floor the inner one being about 20 ins. in diameter and the larger circle about 9 ft. in diameter.

A Patrol is given 12 hollow plastic balls of the type which have holes to impede their flight. The balls can equally well be of size 2½ ins. diameter called gamester balls by the manufacturer or of size 3½ ins. in diameter called teamster balls.

Members of the Patrol distribute themselves round the large circle and the object of the game is to roll the balls from outside the large circle so that as many as possible will be inside the small circle at the end of a strictly observed time limit. On the first occasion two minutes can be allowed but if conditions are favoured a Patrol, after practice, will probably be able to get most of the balls in within a minute. All Patrols as they visit the base will after practice endeavour to establish a minimum record time for getting all the balls in the small circle.

A ball in the area between the two circle circumferences can at any time be snatched out and re-bowled as long as the re-bowling is from outside the large circle, that is the ball must be released from the hand before it crosses the line. A ball counts in if at least half of it is within the small circle as defined by the outer edge of the chalk line. An umpire should quickly announce whether or not a doubtful ball is in or out at any stage in a game.

The game may not be practicable if the floor is too uneven or has a general slope and there should be previous experimentation, if there are any doubts in this respect. It may be possible to select areas of the floor which are suitable. Some irregularities may give an added interest to the game.

It should be appreciated that the holes in the ball assist in bringing it to a stable rest. It will also come to be realised that balls just outside the inner circle can be bumped in by other balls while once a group of balls has been got into the circle others can be brought to rest by bowling them gently against those already in.

The game has spectator attraction and pairs of Patrols can play alternately. The leader in charge of the activity will record best times carefully and succeeding Patrols coming to this particular circuit base will endeavour to beat the shortest time so far established.

154. Clove Hitch in Circle **NCT**

This item is done as part of a circuit for the reason that it is unlikely that there will be room for more than two Patrols to practise at the same time or that a leader will be able to give guidance or make assessment of more than two Patrols at once.

The objective of the activity is for Patrols to tie a clove hitch as quickly as possible round the stave held vertical in the centre of a large circle without any member of the Patrol entering the circle apart from one Scout who lies as close as possible to the floor holding the stave upright.

The size of the circle will depend on the space available but it should be at least 15 ft. in diameter and the length of rope required is roughly three times the diameter of the circle.

A necessary first stage in the activity may be to ensure that the majority of the Troop can tie a clove hitch in usual circumstances. The objective is then explained and the end result demonstrated as achieved by the simple means of going into the circle. Patrols then have a period of about five minutes to try and devise a method of trying the clove hitch in the middle of the circle. During this time Patrols will have their stave and long rope and also some extra staves and some lashing ropes for research.

It is unlikely that any Patrol will in practice be able to devise an effective means of tying the clove hitch round the vertical stave in the centre of the circle and a method, as described below, is demonstrated in outline.

Scout A stands just outside the circle holding the coil of rope in his hand. Scout B goes to the centre of the circle and lies flat on his back holding the stave vertical. Scout C takes the free end of the coil and runs clockwise round the circle to a point opposite Scout A and stands about 4 ft. out from the circumference. Scout A then runs anti-clockwise round the circle carrying the coil of rope and tensioning the rope against the stave. As Scout A approaches Scout C, Scout C raises the end of the rope he is holding so allowing Scout A to pass under the rope. Scout A continues round to his original position. As Scout A reaches his original position Scout D grasps the rope and stands upon it about 4 ft. out from the circumference forming a tight diameter. Scout D then shifts his grip 4 ft. along the rope and stands up producing a 4 ft. vertical length of rope from his foot to his hand.

Meantime Scout A continues anti-clockwise round the circle letting out rope as he goes. This time as he approaches Scout C, Scout C kneels down so allowing Scout A to pass over the rope being held by Scout C. Scout A continues and when he reaches Scout D, Scout A passes through the loop which Scout D is holding with his foot and his hand. As soon as Scout A has passed through the loop Scout D releases the rope completely and the part being held by Scout A is rapidly pulled taut to form the clove hitch.

Although perhaps sounding a little complicated in description the routine is relatively simple and can be rapidly learnt by a Patrol. The operation can be done at the run and times of under 30 seconds should be achieved.

Some force may be exerted on the stave in the centre and if available a second Scout can be used to hold the stave upright. Assuming the Patrol Leader is engaged in directing, the activity done in this way has the attraction of occupying six members of a Patrol.

155. Rolling Hitch in Circle **NCT**

If clove hitch tying as described immediately above has been successfully completed the activity can if desired be extended to the tying of the rolling hitch.

The set up and method is the same as for the clove hitch except that Scout A carrying the rope coil makes two circuits passing under the end of the rope held by Scout C before making the final circuit passing over the rope held by Scout C and passing through the loop held by Scout D.

It should be noted that provided the turns are correctly made round the stave they will, in the case of the clove hitch, always automatically pull together to form the knot however slack they may have been at any stage. This is not the case in respect of the rolling hitch. If the second turn is not kept reasonably taut and kept at an angle upwards against the standing part of the rope (being held by Scout C) the second turn may fall below the first turn with the result that the turns do not tighten to form a rolling hitch. The fault is recognised by a single diagonal lying right across the face of the knot instead of as in the rolling hitch there being two diagonals going across parts of the face. It will be found that the two knot forms are inter-changeable without untying.

The making of the rolling hitch is an interesting extension to be done if the making of the clove hitch has been mastered in good time.

156. Advertisement Making **NCTM**

In this activity Patrols have to compose advertisements and record them on tape.

It is a condition that an advertisement is to last between one minute and one and a half minutes and that all members of the Patrol are to take part.

Assuming that two Patrols together are visiting the circuit base then the recording time must be equally divided between the Patrols and this is aided by each Patrol having to prepare and record two advertisements one of which is to be for some imaginary product and one for joining your Scout Troop.

It is necessary, if there are two Patrols, that there be sound separation areas for recording and for composing and practice which may include singing.

It may be thought of interest to play over all the advertisements to all the Troop together at the end of the circuit.

157. Elastic Band and Cane Pioneering **NLTM**

The basic materials for this activity are elastic bands measuring about 1 cm. wide and 10 cms. long and 3 ft. and 4 ft. garden canes.

A small scale use of these materials is described in the multi-project Making the Greatest (No. 85) but interest in elastic band

and cane pioneering develops from their use for a relatively large scale construction requiring of the order of 250 x 3 ft. canes, 130 x 4 ft. canes and 700 elastic bands.

As a first step it is necessary to learn the method of use of the elastic bands as a lashing. One end of a band is placed over the end of a cane and then the whole band is wrapped in double thickness round two canes with the other end being out over the end of the same or a different cane. This method is not practicable where there is no end of cane available as for example in the centre diagonal lashing position of a trestle. Fortunately these situations do not arise very often and a tie in the position may not be particularly necessary anyway. If it is considered essential the two canes can be brought together by simple tying with two bands linked together or with a broken band.

A suitable construction could be a self-standing gateway with towers at each side about 9 ft. high and 3 ft. square. On top of which is put a box-built horizontal 12 ft. long. The basic method of construction is to make a large number of trestles using the 4 ft. canes as diagonals and to put the trestles together to form boxes which are joined together.

If it is assumed that two Patrols will be involved then each can make a tower and half the horizontals with just a few bands needing to be put on at the end to bring the two parts together.

A considerable degree of engineering organisation is required by Patrol Leaders. It should be noted that a little time is required for demolition and pulling the canes out of the bands. Topline ability would in fact be required to complete a project of this scale in a circuit base period of 25 minutes.

Alternatively this activity can done done by all the Troop together with each Patrol making one or more boxes which can then be quickly joined up.

158. Guide Badge (Circuit) **NLTM**

An activity of learning of street names in the neighbourhood with a competition is described in No. 48 and it is suggested that this be followed up with arrangements for Scouts to gain the Guide badge. It may be preferred, and it would be entirely suitable, for this activity to be done as a circuit item.

159. Method of Moving Injured Persons Without Stretcher (Circuit) **ALTV**

This is considered as a training subject with follow up activities in No. 44.

A time of 25 minutes or so in a circuit will allow all six methods referred to, to be covered fairly fully. In order to give full scope for practice it is to be preferred that there are two Patrols in each group in the circuit.

160. Cooking Activities (Circuit) **NLTMKV**
Various cooking activities can make a useful circuit item especially if there is insufficient equipment for the whole Troop to do the activity simultaneously. Numbers of the items described in Chapter XIV on cooking are very suitable for inclusion in a circuit.

161. Badge Scheme Progress **NLTV**
At this stance the progress which Scouts are making in their Awards is reviewed. It provides an excellent opportunity for people to be encouraged to complete the various stages. There should be leaders present who will help with instruction and assessment.

162. Incident in Circuit **AIMV**
The Incident Journey described in Chapter XVII is itself a supreme example of a circuit programme. It may be thought that one of the individual incidents described in that chapter could usefully be an item at a stance in a Troop meeting circuit type programme though it may not be practicable if two Patrols are visiting the stance together.

163. Volley Ball **ALT**
This is an excellent game which should be played according to the official rules as far as conditions allow. It is not practicable to play the game in low-roofed halls.

The game does require some playing ability and initially at least some Scouts may have difficulty in playing to a standard that will give a reasonably good game. The purpose of including Volley Ball as a circuit activity is so that everyone will learn the rules and by intensive instruction and practice for 25 minutes a standard will be reached which will enable the game to be included in the Troop repertoire of end of meeting team games.

164. Sound Identifications (Circuit) **NCTM**
This competition is fully described in No. 107. The activity is fairly short but is one which is probably best done by only one or two Patrols together. It sometimes happens that an additional activity is required at a circuit stance to make up to the necessary time at other stances and the inclusion of sound identifications can be a good way of providing this.

CHAPTER XIV

COOKING ACTIVITIES

Cooking can be done in a number of forms as a popular and interesting activity at Troop meetings.

An essential requirement is that there should be adequate participation by all members of Patrols. There is for example little point in issuing to a Patrol of six or seven Scouts merely one stove and one cooking utensil which at most can involve two or three Scouts while the others, quite understandably, because there is nothing for them to do, engage in personal activities perhaps of an unhelpful nature.

If stoves or other cooking equipment is limited then consideration should be given to having the activity as part of a circuit (See Chapter XIII). Some Troops will have access to a kitchen and the circuit arrangement will particularly apply if it is intended to use a gas or electric oven.

It will often be appropriate to award inter-Patrol points for quality of cooking. It is worth warning that cooking activities can readily over-run time especially if preparations are inadequate and time-economy procedures are not followed.

Cooking activities are in fact excellent for developing organisational abilities as will particularly apply in the preparation of a Patrol meal. Priority must always be given to the item which is going to take the longest to prepare. There is for example little point in giving attention to some gooseberries which will require only a minute or two of stewing when there is a dixie full of potatoes which has to be got to the boil and boiled for 25 minutes.

It is often practicable for Scouts to carry out cooking on stoves in the Headquarters and in this case the objective is to prepare high quality food for enjoyable eating. A particular use of the activity is for the Scouts to learn basic cooking methods, irrespective of source of heat, with the intention that the practice will be of great value to quality cooking on wood fires at camp. Small butane stoves are of little value for cooking for more than one or two people. Paraffin pressure stoves on the other hand can provide heat virtually the equivalent of a gas ring.

Attention must be given to having plates and cutlery for eating the food and to having a refuse container for each Patrol and suitable clearing up facilities. Especially if washing up facilities are limited it will probably be preferable to use disposable cardboard plates.

The making of Shrove Tuesday pancakes is described in some detail in the section immediately below as an example of cooking with stoves.

165. Shrove Tuesday Pancakes **NLMK**

This cooking activity is appropriately carried out on the Troop meeting night nearest to Shrove Tuesday.

It is essential to ensure adequate individual participation and two frying pans and two stoves are required per normal sized Patrol. Especially if containers are not full small butane stoves may be found to give inadequate heat and at least one paraffin pressure stove, or stove giving equivalent heat, should be available per Patrol. The assembly and lighting of a paraffin pressure stove provides additional occupation for Patrol members. Frying pans should be of a thick or non-stick type. A small amount of cooking fat should be melted in the pan but not enough to have the effect of frying the pancake.

The pancakes are made from a plain flour and milk mix which should be sufficiently thin to run out to give a pancake seven inches or more in diameter and about one eighth of an inch thick. One small dixie or a bowl with spoon for the preparation of the mix is sufficient for each Patrol. A flip is required for each frying pan and the pancake is ready for turning when light brown areas appear on the underside.

The primary objective of the activity is to provide a tasty item of food which will be enjoyed by everyone present but each Patrol can also exhibit with one pancake ability to turn the pancake by tossing. Care must be taken before tossing that the whole area of the pancake is free from any adhesion to the frying pan. Frying pans with collapsible handles are unsuitable for tossing pancakes.

Especially if washing up facilities are limited it is best if the pancakes are served on cardboard plates. The pancakes should be sprinkled with sugar and lemon juice and rolled up and eaten with a knife and fork. A refuse container should be available for each Patrol and a bowl of hot washing up water and a drying cloth at least between two Patrols.

If equipment is limited then this activity can quite well be done as part of a circuit (See Chapter XIII).

166. Mixed Grill Cooking **NLMKV**

All or some of bacon, egg, mushrooms, tomato, saute potato and sausage are to be fried to high quality on stoves to be available for everyone. Potatoes boiled beforehand should be supplied for the saute potato. Pointing includes the extent of non-breaking of egg yolks.

167. Chinese Cooking **NLMKV**

This requires a person with some elementary knowledge of Chinese cooking. Some instruction will be required and also perhaps some special equipment. For this reason it will probably best be done as part of a circuit. Time is unlikely to allow Patrols to cook their own rice which should be available from a ready cooked supply after explaining how the rice would be cooked in camp.

168. Dessert Cooking **NLMKV**

Milk puddings are often poorly cooked in camp. Patrols prepare a small dixie full of custard and also stewed fruit after instruction.

169. Baking **NLMKV**

This can be done as part of a circuit if the Troop has access to a gas or electric oven. Currant buns can be made in the oven while pancakes are made on the top burners. A difficulty in the activity can be lack of individual participation especially if two Patrols at a time have to go to the stove.

An alternative arrangement, if there are four or more Patrols, is for two Scouts to be detached from each Patrol for a period of the Troop meeting for the cooking activity. Three pairs might make currant buns in the oven and three pairs pancakes on the burners and on completion return to the Troop room carrying high quality bakery for their Patrols. Time for the activity can be minimised by using ready made baking mixes.

170. Cooking with Almonds **NLMK**

A most successful and interesting form of miniaturised cooking can be carried out using burning almonds as the source of heat with the advantage that the activity can be done in the Troop room by all Patrols simultaneously.

An almond is impaled on a piece of wire and then lit. It is found that considerable flame and a remarkable amount of heat is generated due to the high oil content of the seed.

Small frying pans can be readily made from wire and aluminium foil. A suitable weight of wire is 1 mm. tying wire (guage 19) and a length of about 26 ins. is required for each frying pan.

A circle of about 4 ins. diameter is made in the middle of the wire and the two ends then twisted together to give a handle about 6 ins. long. The circle is then covered as tightly as possible with a piece of aluminium foil about 5 ins. square.

A small piece of cooking fat should be put into the pan. It is found that a full-sized almond will burn vigorously for about 2½ minutes and this is just long enough to cook a piece of bacon. Also very suitable to cook on the pan are small thin sausages. A second almond may be needed for sausage cooking.

The almonds should be put on to pieces of wire about 8 ins. long. It should be noted that the almonds are not conveniently lit with a match and that each Patrol should have a lighted candle which will ignite an almond in about 15 seconds. 8 in. lengths of wire are also used to make two pronged forks for turning and eating the food.

At least initially it is probably best that Scouts operate in pairs with one holding the frying pan and turning the food while the other moves the flaming almond to give an even spread of heat. It is also possible however for the pans to be projected over the edge of a table, bench or box and held in position by an object such as a shoe or a book resting on the handle. Great care must be taken that the aluminium foil is not punctured and if this does happen the foil must be renewed before use of the pan is continued.

It is important that each Patrol is provided with a refuse container for burnt out almonds and for the final disposal of the equipment. It should be noted that the flame is very sooty and for this reason there cannot be direct cooking in the flame. A heavy layer of soot forms on the underside of pans and care must be taken that this does not cause mess.

The main purpose of the activity is to demonstrate what can be done with what at first sight may seem a very limited supply of heat and also to prepare tasty cooked food which will be enjoyed by everyone present. In these circumstances a Patrol competition may seem rather secondary but it is worthwhile for one or two leaders to devote themselves to assessing that quality of the cooking. A method can be for each Patrol to present for marking out of five their best specimens of bacon and sausage. These may be their first productions but they can afterwards produce other specimens if they think they are of better quality. One leader can mark bacon and one sausage. Marks can also be given for quality of clearing up.

The activity is best started by a very quick demonstration. Supplies of 26 in. and 8 in. wire lengths are best cut with pliers beforehand and it is probably also best to have ready the 5 in.

squares of aluminium foil. Bacon, sausages and cooking fat are conveniently given out to Patrols wrapped in aluminium foil. Almonds at the rate of four per person should be adequate to cook a piece of bacon and a sausage each, but there should be a reserve supply. A two ounce packet contains about 50 almonds.

A further item which can be cooked either on the same or a future occasion is a damper about 1½ ins. in diameter. Because of the small scale of the operation it is more convenient if the damper mix consisting of self-raising flour and milk is made centrally and given out to Patrols in disposable cups. A little cooking fat is put in the pan and the small amount of damper mix added with a dessert-spoon. Cooking time is about two minutes each side.

171. Cooking with Candles NLMK

This activity can be carried through both in method and in items cooked in virtually the same way as cooking with almonds as described immediately above except that the heat comes from a burning candle instead of a burning almond.

As in the case of the almonds people may be surprised at the amount of heat generated by a candle.

Because of the similarity, almond cooking and candle cooking must have good separation in the Troop programme probably of at least two years. On account of the greater degree of novelty, almond cooking has perhaps a slight edge on candle cooking, and for this reason it may be preferred only to do almond cooking.

172. Cooking without Utensils NLMKOV

Troops which are fortunate enough to have ground in the reasonably near vicinity where fires can be lit can carry out cooking without utensils as a Troop meeting activity. This is something which can also be done at camp but it is possibly less popular there since, unless one is engaging in some special survival type exercise, there is a feeling that one wants to do the best one can under the conditions without making things deliberately more difficult by not using cooking utensils.

A factor to be considered is whether or not aluminium foil should be used. It can be argued that aluminium foil is really a utensil and can be used to make pots and a frying pan. It is probably best if aluminium foil is not available for a cooking without utensil activity but that it be used for a separate cooking with aluminium foil activity as described immediately following.

There will need to be a fire for each Patrol and enough items must be cooked to keep all Patrol members occupied. Several leaders will be required to give inter-Patrol points for each item produced and for final cleaning up. Information on cooking without utensils is given in 'The Fun of Scouting'. The following might be required to be produced by each Patrol in a cooking without utensils session.

Egg: Cooked in an inch thick layer of soaked newspaper.

Kipper: Cooked on racquet made with green twigs.

Baked potato: Covered in hot embers for about half an hour.

Australian damper: Thick self-raising flour and water mix is made into a sphere about 2 ins. in diameter which is wrapped in several layers of wet sycamore leaves and placed in hot embers for about a quarter of an hour. Sugar from the sycamore leaves imparts a sweetness to the damper.

Toast: Slices of toasting bread are laid on green-twig forks and held horizontally over a fire preferably at a part free from smoke. Butter or margarine should be available for spreading on the toast. Toast making can become extremely popular at camp sometimes resulting in a large increase in bread consumption.

Twist: A stiff dough is made of self-raising flour and water with a pinch of salt. The end of a green stick about 1¼ ins. in diameter is peeled and a snake of dough about ¾ ins. thick is wrapped in a spiral round the pre-heated stick and baked over the fire. The twist should slide off when cooked. Serve with jam.

173. Cooking with Aluminium Foil **NLMKOV**

This is an improvised form of cooking which can suitably be carried out on wood fires though it is suggested as a separate activity from Cooking without Utensils. It is to be noted that the use of aluminium foil is specifically excluded when cooking without utensils for the Backwoodsman badge.

There is a novelty in using aluminium foil for cooking but as it can readily be fashioned into pots or made into a frying pan using twigs there is less scope for initiative and for variety than in pure cooking without utensils.

Apart from boiling and frying the main use of the foil is to cover food in order to reduce burning while cooking. Suitable items for a Patrol to cook for this activity might be a sausage, piece of bacon and piece of kipper which would probably be fried, and an egg, baked potato and Australian damper which can be cooked as described under Cooking without Utensils except that in each case an outer covering of foil is applied after preparation for cooking.

Aluminium foil is a particularly unsightly form of litter and there must be careful cleaning up at the end of the activity.

174. Cooking with Charcoal NLMKOV

Cooking with charcoal as the source of heat may be novel and intriguing to many Scouts.

The activity can be carried out on a varying scale using tins with large numbers of holes gashed in the bottom and sides. A biscuit tin about 9 ins. square and 5 ins. deep can provide a good cooking fire for a small Patrol but enough to heat though of limited cooking area will come from a tin 5 ins. in diameter and 5 ins. deep. The tins can handily be mounted on two bricks.

Hardwod lump charcoal is probably the most effective and lighting is conveniently done with a proprietary lighting fluid used as per instructions. Some fanning with a plate or the use of bellows may be necessary to get the charcoal into cooking condition quickly. Charcoal and lighting fluid can be got from many camping shops.

Taking cost into account small sausages are probably the best food item to cook using forks made from 20 in. lengths of 1 mm. tying wire.

In view of the variation which can occur in charcoal and in the receptacles for the fires it will often be desirable to carry out a trial run beforehand of this cooking activity.

Although best done outdoors it is possible to do charcoal cooking on a small scale indoors provided there is adequate ventilation, such as might come from opened emergency doors. The fires can be mounted in metal trays.

175. Rabbit Skinning and Cooking NLMKO

By special ordering rabbits can often be obtained in an unskinned state and the skinning and cooking can provide an interesting activity especially at camp where the rabbits can form the main part of a meal.

The rabbits will normally be obtained slit down the belly and with the gut removed. The feet should be cut off with an axe and with the rabbit laid on its back the skin at the rear end of the slit worked over one rear leg, then over the tail and the other rear leg. Some cutting with a sharp knife may be necessary to get the skin over the tail.

Once the skin is over both rear legs the skinning can be rapidly completed by holding the rear legs in one hand and pulling the skin along the body and off the front legs. The non-expert however, will experience difficulty in skinning the head and it will probably be best to cut off the head at the same time as the feet.

The rabbit is then completely cleaned and washed out, during this process it can be valuable to give a brief anatomy lesson noting that the organs of the abdomen have previously been removed.

One rabbit per Scout would be much in excess of requirement and almost inevitably several Scouts will have to get skinning experience working on the same rabbit.

An attractive camp menu item is rabbit stew. A skinned rabbit is cut into about eight pieces and stewed for about two hours along with carrot, turnip and onion.

An alternative cooking method is to thread a green stick through the length of the skinned rabbit and to spit roast over a brisk fire with frequent turning and basting with cooking fat.

176. Pigeon Cooking **NLMKO**

A supply of unplucked pigeons can commonly be obtained by previous ordering and the cooking of the pigeons can provide an interesting activity normally at camp where as in the case of rabbits they can be a main item of the menu.

The head and legs and long tail and wing feathers are taken off and the pigeon coated in about 1½ ins. of moist clay. The pigeon is then placed in the middle of a well burning fire about 20 ins. in diameter and 15 ins. high and left for about one hour. When the pigeon is fully cooked the feathers will come completely away as the clay is taken off.

It is of primary importance for this activity to ensure that there is in fact a good supply of clay. There may be no clay in the vicinity of campsites on sandy or other well-drained soils.

177. Ice-cream Making **NLMEK**

This is a particularly suitable winter activity to be undertaken on a Patrol basis when good supplies of natural ice are available. The method takes advantage of the fact that there is significant lowering of temperature when salt and ice are mixed together and the demonstration of this and its use to freeze an ice-cream mix is of considerable interest.

A simple method of making an ice-cream mix is to buy ice-cream powder which is reconstituted as per the maker's instructions in a 2 pint aluminium dixie. About 2 liquid ounces of reconstituted mix will provide a reasonable sample per person and the total quantity of just over half a pint for a Patrol of six will freeze reasonably quickly.

Well broken ice is required to the extent of 1½ gallons in a 2 gallon bucket per Patrol and it is best if this is available in a container other than the bucket in which the freezing is going to be done.

About 1½ lbs. of salt (conveniently a 750 gram pack) is required per bucket and about 2½ ounces of salt is well mixed with the ice as each layer of about 1½ ins. is put into the bucket. Gloves are wanted for this operation. It is also quite possible to make an adequate freezing mixture with well compressed snow and salt but it is likely to be slightly less powerful.

The aluminium dixie containing the ice-cream mix is bedded down in the freezing mixture to within about half an inch of the top of the dixie. Very great care must be taken that the ice-cream is not spoilt by the entry of salted ice.

The lowering of temperature quickly becomes apparent by frost formation on the outside of the bucket and the ice-cream mix soon begins to harden on the bottom and sides of the dixie. There should be occasional gentle stirring of the mix with a spoon and in particular the forming ice-cream should be scraped from the inside of the dixie so that other parts of the mix can harden.

It will take about 40 minutes for the ice-cream mix to freeze and during this period Patrols should engage in other activities apart from someone doing the occasional stirring. Twice during the freezing process the dixie should be lifted out, the ice roundabout where the dixie lies well dressed with salt, and the dixie quickly bedded back into the ice. Teaspoons and saucers or paper plates should be available for the serving of the prepared product.

Instead of using a powder ice-cream mix, which has become less generally available in recent years, an extremely high quality ice-cream can be made in reasonable Patrol quantity according to the receipe below:

2 eggs
4 drops of vanilla
2 ozs. of icing sugar (previously weighed out in small bags)
¼ pint (5 ozs.) double cream

An attraction of this recipe is that including the preparation of the freezing mixture all members of the Patrol will be simultaneously involved in different operations. In addition to the aluminium dixie, four small mixing bowls, a saucer and three forks and one dessert spoon are required. However, one pint mugs serve excellently in place of mixing bowls.

The whites and yolks of eggs must be carefully separated. This is done by cracking the egg on to a saucer and then pouring off the white into a mug while restraining the unbroken yolk with a spoon. The yolk is then placed in a second mug. The white of the second egg is poured off into a different mug in case of failure in separation. The second white is then placed with the first white and the second yolk added to the first yolk.

Beat egg whites with fork until stiff. Add icing sugar and beat again until stiff.

In separate mug or bowl beat cream until softly stiff.

Whisk egg yolks in separate mug and add vanilla.

Bring all ingredients together in aluminium dixie and mix gently.

There is a knack in beating egg whites and cream with a fork which the Scouts are unlikely to acquire. All this means however is that the beating process which may be little more than stirring takes longer and up to 15 minutes may be required with Scouts acting in relays. Nevertheless the stiffening of the cream can be sudden and care must be taken that it does not go too hard. There should be warning against loss by spillage during beating.

The receipe mix is frozen in just the same way as the powder mix and Patrols should commence other activities when freezing begins.

An especially high standard of hygiene is called for in ice-cream making since in contrast to much other Scout food preparation there is no sterilisation process by heat.

CHAPTER XV

GAMES AND ACTIVITIES FOR CAMP AND TROOP MEETINGS OUTDOORS

Camp provides the great opportunity to carry out activities which physically are not capable of being done in the vicinity of the Headquarters or which require time well in excess of that available at a Troop meeting.

Among possible camp based activities we can list hill walking, rock climbing, abseiling, archery, canoeing, sailing, pioneering, Scoutcraft items of the badge scheme and very importantly outings to places of interest up to quite some distance from the campsite. It is indeed likely to be desirable that the majority of camp time should be taken up with activities of this kind and there is a considerable literature on these subjects including, almost certainly, on places of interest to visit roundabout any particular site.

In addition, however, to programme items often calling for specialist knowledge or depending on local circumstances there is an important place at camp for games which will tend to be regarded as more of a recreational nature and it is such games which are covered in this chapter.

Wide games are often in very popular demand among Scouts. This is a traditional description given to a game played usually between two teams over sometimes quite a wide area of country providing a good amount of cover to allow undetected movement. Unfortunately wide games in practice can often be disappointing. Sometimes this can be due to over complication with elaborate background plots which are difficult to disentangle from what it is intended to do in practice. Another cause of failure is that the ground over which the game is being played is unsuitable: the area may be too small or too large or provide too little cover or too much. Sometimes the game fails because of lack of contact between sides.

Described below are nine daylight wide games. Three night wide games are given in Chapter XVI. A feature of the games is that they are all simple in concept and will have a conclusion with a winner. Several of the daylight wide games require the wearing of wool lives and to avoid repetition it is worth noting at this point that the proper wearing of these lives is important. The wool must be breakable with reasonable ease and in order to give equality, wool lives should always be tied around the right arm clearly visible between the elbow and the shoulder. When sides are using wools of different colour care must be taken that the wools are of equal breaking strength. A side with a weaker breaking wool is at great disadvantage.

Following wide games there is a miscellaneous collection of outdoor games and activities some of which are more appropriate to a weekly Troop meeting. The chapter concludes with some non-energetic items for use in camp in tents in wet weather or in a rest period.

Another especially worthwhile outdoor activity is the Incident Journey. This is considered to be of such value that it is given separate description in Chapter XVII.

178. Release **ARO**

The ideal area for this simple but effective game is a piece of woodland about 200 yards square which has some cover for hiding and stalking. A den about 5 yards square is marked out with Scout staves in approximately the centre of the area.

The game is played between two sides of equal numbers which can vary from about five up to 20. One side is designated away and one catching and each has a different coloured wool life tied round the right arm clearly visible between the elbow and the shoulder. See chapter introduction on wool lives.

The catching side waits beside the den while the away side has a minute to disperse over the playing area. The catching side then endeavours to catch the away side by breaking their wool lives. The away side may resist capture by endeavouring to break the wool of the catching side. Anyone on either side whose wool is broken must cease play at once and return to the area of the den.

At the den there are leaders issuing new lives to catching and away sides. As soon as he has got a new life a member of the catching side immediately becomes active again. On the other hand a member of the away side on getting a new life must go into the den and only becomes active again if he is released. A release is effected by a live member of the away side entering the den and calling release. On this happening members of the away side who are wearing new lives and are in the den attempt to escape into the main playing area. No member of the catching side may enter the den except for one minute after a release. No player may climb a tree.

The session ends either when all the away side are together in the den caught or, if this has not occurred, after a time limit of 20 minutes. The teams then change round. The winning side is the one which has all the opposing side in the den at once caught in the shortest time or if no side is completely caught the one which has caught the most at the end of the 20 minute period.

179. Besieged Stockade **AROV**

This game has some resemblance to Release described immediately above.

A stockade is marked out about 20 yards square with Scout staves in the middle of the area of good cover about 200 yards square though there is no objection to the area extending beyond this and there is no need for any restricting outer boundaries. If the cover is dense more than four staves may be required to mark the stockade and a mallet is likely to be required. The game is played between two sides of equal numbers which can vary from five up to 20.

One side is named besiegers and one relievers and both sides at the start of the game assemble at the stockade where they are issued with different colour wool lives to be tied in a clearly visible position round the right arm between the elbow and the shoulder. At this stage the relievers have the opportunity to observe how best to get into the stockade.

The relievers are given two minutes to disperse into the surrounding area while the besiegers wait at the stockade. At the end of the two minutes a whistle is blown when all the relievers must be at least 50 yards from the stockade. The relievers then have 15 minutes to get into the stockade without their wool life being broken. The besiegers can seek out and endeavour to break the wool of the relievers anywhere in the playing area. The relievers can protect themselves by breaking the wool of the besiegers. Anyone whose wool is broken is out of play and must return at once to the stockade. Besiegers receive new lives as soon as they return to the stockade and can immediately become active again. Relievers whose lives are broken are out of the game and wait beside the stockade for the end of the round. No besieger may go into the stockade, that is he may not use it as a short cut to intercept approaching relievers.

It can be useful for it to be loudly announced that there are five minutes to go to time up and then that there are two minutes. The sides change round either when all of the relievers are caught or have got into the stockade or at the end of the 15 minute time period. The winning side is the one which gets most relievers into the stockade with their wool lives intact.

A variation in the game is to provide stores which it is particularly important be got into the stockade. The stores are represented by footballs which are given to the relievers at the rate of approximately one per five reliever players. The carriers of the football stores are specifically detailed by the umpire and no other relievers may in any circumstances touch a football. It is best if the footballs are given to robust Scouts of medium to small size.

Although other relievers may not touch the football they may defend the carrier from besiegers. The besiegers can attempt to get possession of a football in any way they can. A carrier of a football who has lost his life must immediately give up the football. Besiegers return footballs which come into their possession to the umpire at the stockade.

A football which is got into the stockade counts four points. A football can be thrown or kicked into the stockade. If the game is being played including footballs then one member of the relieving side is left in the stockade to catch any ball which might otherwise pass through the stockade.

180. Wall Sabotage **ARO**

This game is between two sides of equal numbers and can conveniently be played in a wood containing resonable cover and a fence or wall on one side of which about 100 yards are used per five or six players each side.

Both sides have wool lives and the defenders have to prevent the attackers getting to the wall with supposed explosive charges. At the beginning of the game the attackers must be at least 100 yards out from the wall. Defenders attempt to put attackers out of action by breaking their wool lives. Attackers who elude the defenders and touch the wall with their wool lives intact are considered to have laid an explosive charge and gain one point. Attackers can defend themselves by attempting to break the wool of defenders. Any member of either side whose wool is broken must immediately cease play and proceed to the umpire stationed beside the wall at the middle of the section being used. Defenders are immediately issued with new lives and can then at once become active again. Attackers with broken wool lives remain in the area beside the umpire until the end of the round.

In addition to the supposed explosive charges carried by all attackers specialist attackers at the rate of about one per four on the attacking side carry bombs in the form of a football. The footballs are allotted by an umpire and it is best if they are given to small active Scouts rather than to the largest Scouts. In no circumstances may any member of the attacking side other than the specialist to whom the ball is allotted touch that football but any live member of the attacking side may defend a football carrier. The defenders can get possession of the footballs in any way they can. A football carrier whose life is broken must immediately give up his football. Defenders take footballs they gain to the umpire. The attacking side gains four points for any football which a carrier manages to put into contact with the wall. A football may be thrown or kicked against the wall. An attacker who has touched the wall is out of play. For example he cannot thereafter help to escort in a football carrier or another attacker. A round of the game ends when all the attackers have either got through to the wall or lost their lives or if this has not happened at the end of a 15 minute time limit. The attackers then become defenders either in front of the same wall or assuming conditions are more or less equal in front of a wall at the other end of the wood. The winning side is the one which as attacker gains most points from individuals from getting through counting one each and from footballs getting through counting four each.

As an alternative to a wall the object of sabotage may be a road represented by a path running through the wood or a canal represented by a stream.

181. Strategic Crossing **AIO**

This game is suitably played on an area of ground measuring 300 yards by 200 yards between two sides of about 15 Scouts each though smaller numbers can play in a suitably reduced area. The area may be wholly or partly defined by existing boundaries. If need be Scout staves can be malleted in to complete the marking of the area. The layout of the area for the game and method of playing is best described by reference to the example diagram given below:

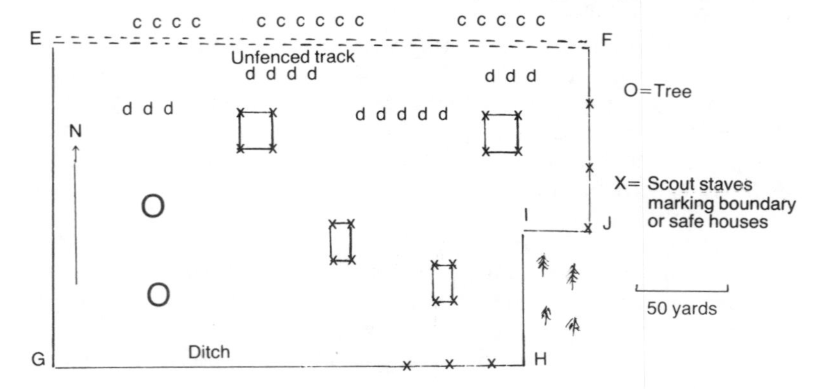

At the commencement of the game the members of the crossing side marked c on the diagram are assembled on or just to the north of the length of track marked EF. These Scouts have to get across the playing area and over the south boundary marked GHIJ formed by a ditch, Scout staves and the edge of a wood without being touched by any of the defenders marked d within a time limit of 15 minutes.

The situation is complicated by the fact that there are a number of safe houses within the playing area in which members of the crossing side cannot be touched. These safe houses may consist of natural features such as the spread of a tree or may be made by using Scout staves to mark out areas about 15 yards square.

The placing and use of safe houses is an important factor in the success of the game which lends itself to all kinds of strategies including feints and various co-ordinated initiatives. It is very good if Patrol Leaders from each side can have separate planning sessions as a tewt (tactical exercise without troops). There is in fact quite some skill in constructing the layout of the area to make a good game and the person doing this must put himself in the place of someone planning to get his Scouts across. A chief umpire and an assistant umpire are required.

The winning side is the one which gets most Scouts across within the time limit. Each side might have two crossing sessions and two defending sessions. Although the normal time limit is 15 minutes the chief umpire may announce that a session will end in two minutes time if it seems there can be no new developments in the play. For example if a few surviving members of the crossing team are in one safe house surrounded by all the defending side then there is no point in everyone having to wait more than two minutes for an attempted breakout. If, however, after breakout the game opens up then the foreshortening can be cancelled.

182. Territory Crossing **ARO**

An example playing area for this game could be a wooded or other piece of ground giving good cover measuring about 500 yards by 800 yards. There are two sides of equal numbers which set out simultaneously from opposite 500 yard ends to reach the boundary at the other end within a time limit which might be 20 minutes in this particular case.

Every Scout who makes the crossing in the time limit gains one point. In addition however, one side is designated interceptors and during the crossing they endeavour to touch as many of the other side as possible. Each member of the non-intercepting side gains an additional point if he makes the crossing without being touched. The sides then make a second crossing with the non-interceptors acting as interceptors. In this way the intercepting will be done in the same direction. If, for example, there are six on each side then a side can get a maximum of six points crossing as interceptors and 12 points crossing as non-interceptors to give a possible maximum of 18 points.

Numbers up to about 20 a side can play each other but in these circumstances it will be better to have a larger area of ground. The giving of the right amount of time for crossing is important and this should be assessed by a leader timing his own crossing at slow walking pace with spare time for intercepting or avoiding interception.

An advantage of merely touching to achieve interception is that it allows small boys more readily to intercept larger ones. If however it is felt that there can be doubts as to whether or not a person has been touched then the side being intercepted wears wool lives. The wool should be of an easily breaking strength. No lives are worn by the intercepting side.

One or two umpires may go with the intercepting side. It is important that there is synchronisation of watches so that sides depart simultaneously from each end.

183. Water Carrying **ARMO**

The object of this game is to carry, or prevent being carried, a water supply across an area of ground.

There are two sides and a suitable playing area for about eight a side might be 150 yards by 60 yards. A reasonable amount of cover is desirable especially so that one cannot see from one end of the area to the other. If there is a lack of natural boundaries these will have to be formed by the malleting in of Scout staves.

Just outside the playing area and at the middle of the 150 yard line there is a four gallon water supply in two buckets. The carrying side assembles by the buckets and each Scout is given a plastic cup.

Following the start of the game the carrying side fill their cups with water and attempt to carry the water across the playing area to the safety of the 150 yard line on the other side. The non-carrying side is dispersed in the playing area to intercept the water carriers. There is no need for players of either side to wear lives since the non-carriers only require to spill the water being carried in the cups. A carrier whose water is spilled merely returns at once to the middle of the start line to renew his supply and try again.

Water receiving buckets are placed on the other side of the playing area just beyond the boundary at each end of the 150 yard length. Water carriers are entirely safe before they cross the start line and can set off from any point they choose along the 150 yard length. Likewise they are safe once they cross any part of the line on the opposite side of the playing area and can then proceed along to empty their cup into a receiving bucket.

It is to be understood that all carriers must make their own way across and that there can be no use of guards though there can be co-ordinated sallies by water carriers. Water carriers who have emptied their water into a bucket return up the side and not across the playing area. Members of the carrying side may only attempt to escape from the non-carrying side and can never play a non-carrier with, for example, the objective of allowing other carriers to cross.

According to conditions the game can develop in different ways. There may be a certain amount of stalking using cover or the game may more take the form of the game Strategic Crossing described earlier in this chapter. In some circumstances success may depend on athleticism with a willingness for the carriers to keep running back and forth.

Each team has a session of being carrier and non-carrier and the winner is the one which gets most water across into the receiving buckets within a given time limit. The time limit will depend on the tempo of the game but is likely to be found best between 10 minutes and 20 minutes.

In addition to buckets for supplying and receiving water, equipment must include a good supply of plastic cups to allow for breakages and a ruler to measure the amount of water transported.

As an alternative to plastic cups it may be practicable to use personal enamel camp mugs. In this case, however, one must beware that undue biasing does not arise from some people using very large mugs. It may also be necessary to arrange for larger supplies of water.

184. Vehicle Ambush **ARMO**

The requirement for this game is a section of quiet private road or track about 500 yards long with reasonably dense cover on either side and a good supply of pine cones. The game requires two sides one designated bandits and one guards with a minimum of about six a side and ideally not more than 15 a side.

The bandits with everyone having about 12 cones each are given about three minutes to take up ambushing positions along the designated length of road. The guards then have 15 minutes to escort the vehicle (or trek cart) from one end of the road length to the other with minimal hits by cones thrown by the bandits.

The vehicle is never driven at more than easy walking pace, say three miles per hour, but the Scout leading the guards can ask the driver to proceed more slowly or to stop the vehicle at any time. No guard may position himself closer than 6 ft. to the vehicle. The guards also carry cones and bandits are put out of play by being hit with a cone thrown by a guard. Guards are not put out of play by being hit with a cone. No bandit may go into a position more than 10 ft. above the ground. Bandits put out of play walk along together as spectators about 20 yards behind the vehicle.

If a trek cart is in use this is pulled by one of the guards. One or two umpires are required to walk beside the vehicle to record hits. No bandit may throw more than one cone simultaneously, that is he cannot throw a handful of cones. Success from the point of view of the guards, is chiefly obtained by sending parties forward on both sides of the road to clear out bandits from undergrowth and shrubbery. It can be surprising how unthoroughly this operation may be done. Bandits may hide some way back from the road, allow the vehicle to pass and then run up from the rear.

Sides change round after each pass along the road. The side securing most hits when bandits is the winner assuming they get the vehicle along in the time. It may be necessary to clear the road of cones at the end of the activity.

185. Lion and Hunters ARO

This game is best played between Patrol sized units in an area giving good cover at least 200 yards square though the game can well be played over a distance of half a mile or more.

The lion side has yellow wool lives and the hunter green wool lives. The lion is wounded and leaves a trial of blood which is represented by pieces of red wool about 2 ins. long dropped approximately every 8 yards.

The lion is given about five minutes start with the hunters unable to view the direction in which the lion has gone. At the end of the five minutes the hunters are taken to the start of the blood trail and endeavour to make up on the lion. At a suitable spot the lion circles back to a concealed position looking over the earlier part of the trail. The lion springs out from its ambush hopefully to take the hunters by surprise. No lions or hunters may go more than 30 yards from the point of ambush and fighting for wool lives continues until only a member or members of one side remains which is declared the winner.

After the first ambush the sides can change over and the new hunters follow the new lion to another ambush. It may well be that another two Patrols can be playing simultaneously in another part of the area. Care must be taken that blood trails do not become inter-mixed.

It is important that trails are not too easy to follow because of excess of red wool or too difficult because of lack of wool. An umpire with the lions can make sure that wool is being dropped in proper quantity. An umpire is needed to start off the hunters. It can be useful if umpires know roughly intended routes so that they can keep the game going should the trail be lost at any stage.

186. Prince Charlie **ARO**

This game gives an opportunity for some of the Patrol Leaders or larger Scouts to take part in an activity working together on their own. A reasonably large woodland or other area with good cover is required.

One of the smallest Scouts in the Troop is designated Prince Charlie and he wears a red wool life. Depending on numbers taking part three or four Patrol Leaders or large Scouts are designated the loyal guards of Prince Charlie. The rest of the Troop is the army of redcoats searching for Prince Charlie. The general leading the army may be one Patrol Leader not forming the guard.

Prince Charlie moves about to the instruction of the guards who are given five minutes to hide Prince Charlie and themselves in the playing area. The redcoats under the leadership of the general have to find Prince Charlie and capture him by breaking his wool life within a suitable time limit. This might be 20 minutes but can be longer if the area is large.

The redcoats and their general have wool lives. The guards have no wool lives. When the redcoats find Prince Charlie they try to get to him against the defence of the guards. If the wool of a redcoat is broken by the guards he must cease play at once and he cannot resume until he has got a new life from a leader stationed close to the scene of action. The essence of the game is whether a concentrated attack by say 20 relatively small Scouts can break through the defence of three or four of the largest Scouts.

The guards can move Prince Charlie about the playing area if they wish and place him in a guardable position though not one which may be virtually impossible of access. Prince Charlie may not be placed in a tree. If it appears that the redcoats are not going to find Prince Charlie than some hints as to his location may be given in order to provide an active conclusion to the game.

187. Camp Cricket **ARO**

It is appropriate to make a reasonably serious approach to this game as for a normal game of cricket. The distinctive features of Camp Cricket are that it can be played on quite rough ground as is commonly experienced at camp and that a game can be completed much more quickly than a standard cricket match; an innings with 11 players can be expected to last not more than 20 minutes.

The pitch is marked out with a crease at each end in a similar way to cricket but with the length reduced to about 18 yards with as smooth a piece of ground as possible being chosen for the running surface. The wickets however in this case consist of single Scout staves hammered firmly into the ground to stand about 4 ft. 3 ins. high and carrying against the top-most section an object such as a 10 pint dixie, a large frying pan or a piece of wood presenting a face to the bowler of roughly 10 ins. square. A batsman is bowled by the hitting of this main part of the wicket or the stave. The bats consist of round or slightly eliptical wood batons about 20 ins. long with the maximum diameter being about 1¼ ins. A mallet handle or a portion of a broken thick Scout stave may be suitable or natural round timber may be available. The same bats are used throughout the match.

Play is with a tennis ball and bowling is underhand. A fundamental rule differentiating the game from normal cricket is that a batsman must run whenever he hits the ball however short may be the hit and however likely that the striking or non-striking batsman may be run-out. As a result far more players are run-out than in normal cricket with great emphasis being put on good fielding and sharp backing up by the non-striking batsman.

In addition to being bowled and run-out a batsman can be out caught, stumped, played on or LBW if in the opinion of the umpire the ball would have hit any part of the wicket if not obstructed by any part of the person of the batsman.

It is desirable that the rules and normal procedures of cricket should be followed as closely as possible with overs of six balls, an umpire at the bowlers end and at square leg and with a field set and changing over much as in ordinary cricket. The batting side sits in a designated pavilion, and scores are carefully logged.

Extras are signalled by the umpire for wides for bowls which are considered out of reach of the batsman either to the side or upwards. Normal no balls are called but because the nature of the ground requires that for reasonable play a bowled ball is in the air as it approaches the batsman a no ball is also called (by the square leg umpire) for any bowl which comes to the ground more than 4 ft. in front of the batsman's crease. No balls and wides do not count as part of the over but to provide for the situation where an occasional boy may not be able to bowl within the required limits of accuracy an over is considered ended if a total of six wides or no balls have been bowled.

Boundaries for four runs or six runs should be instituted according to features such as fences, clumps of bracken or streams which may be round about. Also to provide against any possibility of the ball being lost or becoming inaccessible it is a rule that no more than six runs may be taken from a single strike.

The game can be played from a minimum of about six a side up to a little in excess of the normal 11. In order to maximise participation it is a good rule that when fielding no one may bowl a second over until everyone has bowled one over and similarly no one a third over until everyone has bowled two overs but within these restrictions the captain decides who is bowling next. Also at the end of an innings the not out batsman receives a further maximum six bowls playing single end cricket.

188. Camp Golf — ARMO

At one time this game was commonly played with personal camp plates usually of enamel. The plates would rapidly become damaged and there was also an element of danger from such plates being thrown about.

Camp Golf can now be much more satisfactorily played with plastic discs about 8 ins. in diameter which can be bought for the primary purpose of throwing and catching among persons on the beach or elsewhere and it is well worthwhile acquiring a stock to enable Camp Golf to be played much more attractively. The game should not be played around the campsite and it is a pleasing feature of the game that it can take the players away on a walk of some distance as on a golf course.

The group of players take it in turn to choose "holes" to be hit which can vary from quite short up to 300 yards or so. It may sometimes be necessary to define the hole carefully, for example any part of a tree or the trunk of a tree below the first branch. Other holes might be a bush, a rock or a fence post. Sequence of play generally follows that of normal golf. Care should be taken to avoid the nuisance of discs getting stuck in trees.

The game is worth taking seriously like golf with rounds of nine or 18 holes and with a tournament probably best based on pairs playing each other.

189. Tenniquoit **ARMO**

It is well worthwhile taking the equipment to enable a tenniquoit court to be set up at camp. The court should be of size for play by doubles.

The net which can be made on site from twine should be about 19 ft. long, about 5 ft. 8 ins. high and about 18 ins. deep and go across the middle of the court. Overall the court measures about 40 ft. by 18 ft. with a dead area 3 ft. on either side of the net and a line down the centre making half courts. Lining can be done with twine held down by small metal tent pegs well hammered in.

Serving is from behind the end line starting behind the right hand half court into the half court diagonally opposite. One player has five serves changing from side to side after each serve. The player on the other side in the right hand half court then commences five serves. Two serves and one let per serve are allowed. Points are gained or lost as a result of failing to catch the tenniquoit ring, or the ring going out of court, into the dead area, into the net or into the wrong half court on second serve.

Winners are the first to reach 11 points but with continuation if necessary to win by two clear points. The game merits being played seriously. The court can be used at odd times but a camp tournament can be a worthwhile programme item.

190. Relay Message **ALO**

It will often be possible for this game to be played in the vicinity of the Headquarters.

A circuit course of about 1500 yards is chosen and one Scout from each Patrol goes to stances spaced 200 to 300 yards apart. The number of stances and distance apart will depend on the number of Scouts in Patrols. A verbal message is given which has to be conveyed round the circuit by Scouts running to the next stance ahead where they repeat the message to the member of their own Patrol waiting there.

The message should be relatively simple and might for example be "The Troop is moving camp. Send food, maps, ropes and bagpipe players to the site beside the loch."

It is a good arrangement for the Assistant Patrol Leaders to be the first runners and Patrol Leaders the last runners. The message can be written up on a blackboard in view of the first runners and they then have a further minute to memorise it. The Assistant Patrol Leaders then go outside the building for a formal simultaneous start. Scouts return direct to the Headquarters when they have run their sections.

The position of the Patrol Leaders is noted as they cross the finishing line. They then immediately go to a room on their own to write down the message. The weighting of pointing between speed and accuracy is important. Assuming there are six Patrols then four, three, two and one point can be given for the first four getting round the circuit within an overall time limit of say 12 minutes. The messages as written down by the Patrol Leaders are carefully marked for accuracy out of ten.

191. Kim's Game Matching **AIO**

This is a good Headquarters based activity in the period of light evenings.

A collection is made of around 14 objects which can be found fairly readily within about a quarter of a mile of the Headquarters. No object should have a dimension exceeding 1 ft. A typical collection might be as follows:

Twig of ash	Feather
Piece of gravel	Oak leaf
Leaf of coltsfoot	Piece of cloth
Dandelion flower	Piece of moss
Piece of coal	Bus ticket
Matchbox	Daisy chain
Piece of Newspaper	Piece of string

The object of the game is for each Patrol to make a collection of objects, which is as far as possible identical with the specimen collection, after viewing it for one minute. It is explained that this will be judged by giving one point for every object correctly collected but more importantly, among Patrols, three points will be given for the object most like the original, two points for the second most like and one point for the third most like.

The objects are laid out on the floor or on a table in an area where they can be viewed by two Patrols at a time away from the rest of the Troop. Since the viewing time is so short there will be little delay between the first and last Patrols seeing the objects but later Patrols can be given a few minutes extra at the end of the collecting period. After all Patrols have viewed the objects they are put away carefully in a bag.

No notes may be taken while viewing but as much description as desired can be written down afterwards and the drawing up of a list immediately after viewing is an important first step for the Patrol to take.

A suitable time limit for completion of the collection after viewing is 25 minutes but the time can be varied according to size of Patrols, number of objects and distance over which it is thought objects will have to be collected. It must be emphasised that no objects will be accepted after the expiry of the time limit and that everyone must be back by that time.

The judging of the competition is an important part of the activity and can give considerable interest. Patrols accumulate their collection in Patrol corners and while this is going on a block of boxes for judging items is drawn out in the middle area of the floor. Each box is 1 ft. square and if there are 14 objects and six Patrols the block consists of 15 squares lengthwise along the hall and seven squares downwards as shown below:

Object Patrol														
Woodie														
Gannet														
Owl														
Swift														
Hawk														
Eagle														

Patrol names are written in the squares down the left hand side of the block and on expiry of time the objects are taken from the bag and placed in any order in the top row of squares. One member from each Patrol then brings out their objects and places them beneath the specimen objects in the row of boxes opposite their Patrol name. Patrols then gather round, but well clear of the block, to view the judging.

The first stage of judging is to give one point for every object correctly collected. Complete accuracy is not necessarily required. For example a point will be given to all Patrols with a twig and a yellow flower even if they are not ash and dandelion. The correct objects are totalled and the number put in the left hand box for each Patrol.

For the next stage of assessment two judges operate starting at each end of the block. The judge compares the objects in the Patrol boxes with the object in the specimen box and decides which is to receive three points for being most like the specimen, which two points and which one point. These points when awarded are chalked in the Patrol object boxes.

It adds considerably to interest if a judge gives reasons for assessments especially in close cases. For example he may say that a leaf is too large, a matchbox not struck enough or a bus ticket is too clean. These comments can attract cheers or calls of disapproval.

On completion of judging the points for similarity are totalled for each Patrol and written in left hand boxes where they are added to the points for number of objects to give a grand total. Including the very worthwhile marking the activity will take 50 minutes to one hour.

192 Holes in the Road **ALO**

A large number of authorities are responsible for services on, below or above the road and pavement surface. The object of the activity is to note the evidence of all these services. The title of the activity comes from the fact that many of the authorities dig up the road.

A quiet section of road probably about 300 yards long in a built-up area is selected which Patrols visit and draw in the items on a plan. It is best to give out blank plans of the road in which the width is exaggerated in relation to the length so that items can be drawn in more readily. It is also useful to divide the plan into two or three parts so that Patrols can split up with Patrol sub-units covering different sub-sections of the road. In these circumstances a time limit of 15 minutes should be sufficient. Patrols hand in completed plans for assessment with Patrol names written on.

Among services noted may be water, gas, electricity, telephones, sewers, surface drainage, street lighting, road name, bench mark and pillar box.

193. Tree Registration **AIO**

This is an inter-Patrol competition in which Scouts have the opportunity to demonstrate their ability to climb and to identify trees. An area of well grown woodland is required where it is permitted to climb trees and where preferably there are trees of several different species.

The background to the activity is that Patrols can register a tree in their name provided a member of their Patrol can climb the tree and the objective is to achieve maximum registration points. A tree is defined as climbed if a Scout has all of his person in the tree at least 10 ft. from the ground.

There is additional advantage to be obtained from registering as many different species of tree as possible. The first tree of a particular species climbed counts five points, the second four points, the third three points, the fourth two points, the fifth one point and every tree of the species in excess of the fifth as one point. All Patrols should be issued with a form on which trees climbed can be listed and points recorded. Given below is an example completion of a form where a total of 18 trees of three different species were climbed to give a total of 45 registration points.

Patrol...............................

Name of Tree Species	Points per specimen registered						
	1st 5	2nd 4	3rd 3	4th 2	5th 1	In excess of 5th 1	Total points
Example Ash	5	4					9
Example Elm	5	4	3	2	1	1	16
Example Lime	5	4	3	2	1	11111	20
Example Total	15	12	6	4	2	6	45

It would be expected that there will be more than three different tree species and there should be at least 12 lines on the form. In order to be sure that the method of pointing is understood it is helpful to reproduce an example section as given above at the top of the form.

The completion of the form is in fact done by a registrar who accompanies each Patrol and who is an Assistant Patrol Leader from another Patrol. The registrar carries a Scout stave and with this and his own reach upwards he is able to ensure that the tree is climbed to the required height. It is helpful if there are leaders in the area who can give information on tree species if this is necessary.

More than one tree at a time can be being climbed by a Patrol and it is a job of the Patrol Leader to ensure that there is a continuing supply of climbable trees. Trees can be climbed and registered which have already been climbed by another Patrol. Scouts can assist each other to get up a tree but it is best that the use of ropes, ladders or other equipment be not allowed. If the area contains copse growth or other insubstantial trees then in order to avoid possible damage, it is likely to be desirable to impose a minimum diameter below which trees may not be climbed.

The winner is the Patrol which collects the maximum registration points within a time limit which might be half an hour.

194. Gaining Ground **ARO**

This game is played with a football between two teams of about six a side on a piece of ground roughly the size of a football pitch or a bit larger if there are powerful kickers playing. Marking out of the ground with Scout staves may be necessary.

At the start teams occupy their own halves of the playing area. Each side kicks the ball alternately and the object of the game is to get the ball over the opponents goal line.

Each side takes it in turn to kick off which is by a place kick 20 yards back from the centre of the playing area. The opposite side attempts to field the ball as far forward as possible. The player fielding the ball then makes a return kick which can be a punt or a place kick from the point where the ball is brought to rest except that this may not be in advance of where the ball is first touched. The punt will be preferred where a quick return is likely to be advantageous. Alternate kicking continues until the ball goes over a goal line.

A ball which goes out of play over a side line is brought back to a point 10 yards in from where it is considered to have gone out of play. The winner is the side which makes most scores over their opponent's goal line within a time limit.

195. Athlete Badge **ALO**

The taking of the tests to gain the Athlete badge by all the Scouts can form the basis of a very worthwhile outdoor Troop meeting provided sufficient playing field type ground is available.

Requirements for the badge including the detail of points gained for varying performance in events by Scouts of different ages should be reproduced and issued to all Scouts at the beginning of the meeting. A simple method of organisation is to split the ten events among six bases. Although only three events are used to qualify for the badge there is no reason why the Scouts should not do more with their best three results, within the rules, counting towards the badge. It can be of interest to try what may be a new event such as putting the shot.

Assuming six Patrols, one Patrol goes to each base and there is movement round every 15 minutes. Each Scout must attempt at least one event at each base. It is convenient if each Scout has a card with the names of the events down the side and a space for inserting the points gained. Scouts qualify for the badge if they gain sufficient total points for their age from any three qualifying events.

If there are less than six Patrols then there will always be one or more bases vacant and a lesser number of leaders will be required. In addition to qualifying for the Athlete badge it is useful to run the activity as a Patrol competition. This has the advantage of giving a reason for participation by any Scouts who have already gained the badge. In the competition points are totalled for the six events in which each Scout has done best and the average of these totals calculated for each Patrol.

196. Naval Battle **NCO**

This game is played in pairs. It is particularly suitable for use in wet weather or a period of relaxation in camp.

The playing blocks and the rules are given below. It is suggested they are reproduced together on the same sheet of paper or card to number required. India-rubbers will be required to allow repeated use.

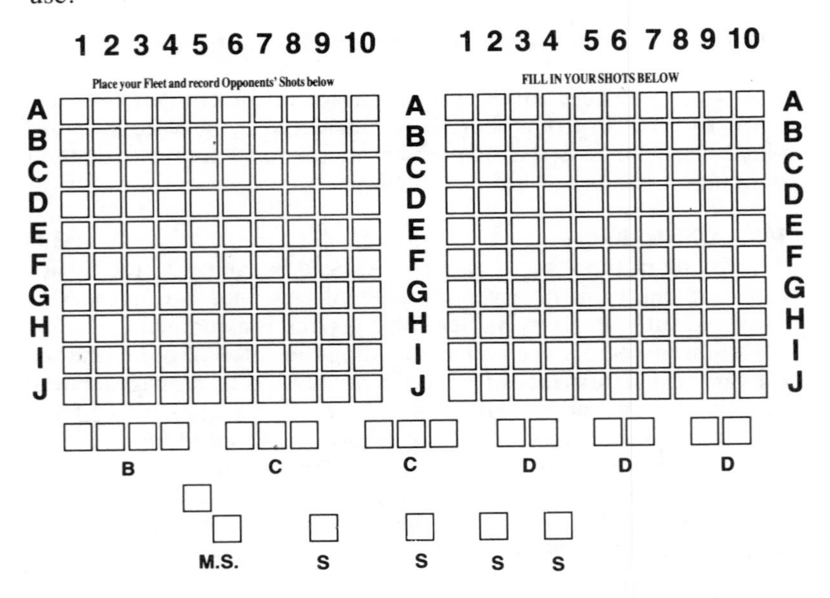

Method of Play

Two persons each with a card place their fleet at random on the left-hand block, giving the correct number of small squares as shown on the Key, i.e., One Battle Ship (4), Two Cruisers (3), Three Destroyers (2), One Minesweeper (2 diagonally) and Four Submarines (1). The ships can either be placed across or up-and-down, and a space must be left all round between them, but may be placed against any of the margins.

The object is to sink the opponent's ships taking turn about with three shots each time. Call out your shots, such as, J.3, A.5, D. 10, and the opponent marks these on the left-hand block of his card by a 1 for each of the first turn, 2 for each of the second turn, and so on. He then reports, at the end of the time only, if you have recorded any hit or sunk any ship, but does not say which particular shot of the three has found a mark. If two hits are made on the same ship at one turn the opponent does not necessarily disclose this, i.e., he only requires to report thus, "You've hit a Cruiser. You've hit a Cruiser." When shooting, mark your shots on the right-hand block of your card, and when any hit is reported record same in the appropriate place in the Key, i.e., if during your third round you "Hit a Battle Ship" and "Hit a Destroyer," put a 3 in the first square of the "B," also a 3 in the first square of any of the three "D's" in the Key.

The game is continued until one of the fleets is completely wiped out.

197. Competitions in Tents **NCMOV**

It is most useful to have a supply of puzzles and quizzes which can be used to mount a large-scale tent-based inter-Patrol competition on a very wet day in camp.

Suitable puzzles and quizzes are often to be found in magazines while there are numbers of books of puzzles. Among these are the Piccolo Puzzle Books and, especially recommended, the Handbook of Indoor Games and Contests by Darwin A. Hindman published by Edmund Ward. Several specialist Scout quiz books are available.

In a large-scale competition it will be desirable to produce about six items so that all members of a Patrol can be fully occupied and altogether there should be so much to do that no Patrol will complete everything in the time allowed which might be one hour. In some instances to ensure that an item is fully understood it may be useful to give the answer to one question. There will be a significant (probably consumable) prize for the winning Patrol tailing down to something very nominal for the last Patrol.

An in-tent inter-Patrol competition might consist of the

following, the first four items being from the Handbook of Indoor Games and Contests.

1. Chapter 9, No. 12. Buried birds. e.g. Do you recognise a gleam in her eye? Answer eagle.
2. Chapter 9, No. 38. What tree? e.g. What is the neatest tree? Answer spruce.
3. Chapter 9, No. 40. What letters? e.g. What two letters mean vacant? Answer M T.
4. Chapter 17, No. 11. Reconstruction of a letter T cut into four pieces. This can be conveniently done by supplying the cut pieces on gummed paper.
5. A quiz with about 30 questions on the history of the Scout movement and perhaps the history of the Group.
6. Using not more than one Scout stave and three knotting ropes tie as many knots as can be found in particular handbooks. The books may be consulted.

CHAPTER XVI

NIGHT GAMES

There can be popular demand for a night wide game. It has to be recognised however that fast movement and vigorous encounters in the dark do carry quite some risk of injury. Wide games in the dark should therefore be of a kind which avoids the need for either of these actions and should instead depend on slow stalking which may not be practicable in daylight because of lack of cover in a particular area.

At the beginning it is worth noting that an essential requirement for a night wide game may be that the area of play is sufficiently dark. In conditions of moonlight or even just clear sky visibility may be such that there is little differentiation between playing the game in daylight. In the northern part of Great Britain it is unlikely to become sufficiently dark in the months May to July for a wide game requiring reasonable darkness and for this reason the activity is particularly suitable as a means of filling a part of the long dark evening at a September weekend camp.

Care must be taken that there is no damage to crops or fences or disturbance to livestock. It may be necessary to warn local people that a night game is going to take place and Scouts should be advised to bring spare torch batteries to camp.

198. Night Sabotage **AROV**

This game takes the form of previously described Wall Sabotage (No. 180). The attacking side goes out into an area of reasonable cover to a distance of at least 50 yards from a section of wall of 100 yards or more length and have to creep up and touch the wall without being intercepted and identified by the defenders.

No wool lives are worn. Both sides carry torches though these will tend to be used only by the defenders and an attacker is considered to be identified and captured when he is illuminated sufficiently for his name or a description of his clothing to be called out. There will be a time limit of 15 minutes. The sides change round and the winner is the one which gets most to touch the wall during its attacking session. Equally well the achievement of sabotage can be counted by touching a fence or reaching or crossing a path, stream or ditch. Several umpires may be required. Attackers who are caught or who have got through gather beside the chief umpire at an indicated spot.

The success of the game is dependent upon having adequate darkness, having the right amount of cover and having the right number of players in relation to the length of fence or other objective for sabotage.

199. Night Attack **AROV**

Depending on conditions being suitable the attackers in this game have to get into the campsite or part of the campsite. Attackers are intercepted as described in Night Sabotage (No. 198). It may be necessary to define some boundaries by the use of Scout staves and loosely tied twine. Here attackers who are caught or get through will probably be able to congregate round a fire while waiting for the end of the session.

A variant is that suitably located tents can be designated to be blown up. Each of the attackers carries a bomb which has been made beforehand and can consist of moss or bracken leaves tightly tied up into a ball with twine. Tents to be bombed have a bright light in them partly to allow the tents to be found and partly so that umpires can see that tents have in fact been hit. Attackers can throw their bombs at tents from any distance out they choose. A point is given for every hit on a tent with a bomb and for every attacker who gets into the campsite unidentified.

200. Night Hike Interception **AROV**

This is a form of night wide game involving a short night hike. Indeed the game can provide something of a focus for the hike. The game has some resemblance to Territory Crossing (No. 182).

Two points are selected about a mile apart. There should be reasonably rough ground between the points and it is in fact convenient if one of the points can be the campsite. For purpose of illustration the campsite is termed A and the other point B.

There are two sides of equal numbers and one side is either conveyed or walks to point B. Both sides leave their points simultaneously and everyone who reaches the other point within a time limit which might in this case be 40 minutes scores a point. As in Territory Crossing one side is designated the interceptor. While making the crossing the interceptor side endeavours to identify individuals in the other side by shining a torch on them. An umpire walking with the interceptors assesses the degree of identification.

If desired the hike can be repeated with the other side acting as interceptors and an umpire again making an assessment of the degree of identification. Points for identification are added to points for crossing within time limit. It may however not be particularly wished to repeat a hike over the area and in this case an umpire can award points to both sides on the extent to which they achieved or avoided identification.

The activity may require quite some skill in map reading. Patrol Leaders in particular may have to memorise the route they are going to take. There should be defined limits on the width of the corridor which may be used by the two sides. The width however may be quite great. Sides can select their own routes and there may well be no interceptions. Everyone should have a torch though success in the game will often depend on not using torches.

It will probably not be desirable for individuals to proceed independently and units of Patrol size are very appropriate. If there are two Patrols per side then they can go by different routes with an umpire with each of the intercepting Patrols.

In other conditions the game can be based on a mile long length of track which has good cover on one or both sides. In this case the non-intercepting side can take cover at an appropriate spot and wait for the intercepting side to pass.

201. Morse Code Night Games **ALOV**

Night games involving the use of morse code are described under No. 43.

CHAPTER XVII

INCIDENT JOURNEY

202. Incident Journey AIMOV

The incident journey is probably the most potent Scouting activity for the learning of leadership and of ability to operate as a team in the achievement of a desired end.

Normally one would expect the incident journey to be carried out at camp. The general principle of the activity is that each Patrol visits a number of stations at each of which instructions are given to deal with some kind of incident within a time limit. Each incident must take the same time to deal with which can suitably be 15 minutes and five incidents is an appropriate number with the result that the whole activity lasts 1¼ hours. The 15 minutes includes time for clearing up and re-setting the incident if necessary as well as time for moving on to the next incident. In less experienced Troops it will almost certainly be preferable to allow 20 minutes per incident and in this case the timings given in the incidents later described in detail should be increased by 5 minutes.

The placing and distance apart of the incident stations will much depend on ground configuration. It will usually be desirable that incidents are out of sight of each other. Commonly with distance between 100 to 200 yards the actual time of movement from one incident to another will be negligible. It is generally undesirable to make the finding of the next incident station a matter of puzzle solving since arriving late at incident stations, or not arriving at all, can cause great disruption and can result in quite excessive points penalties. If desired, direction finding can be the subject of one particular incident. It is best if each Patrol is taken by a judge from a general assembly point to their first incident station.

The ideal may be considered five Patrols simultaneously visiting five different incident stations each with its own judge. However, if there are less than five Patrols there is no reason why one or more incidents cannot be vacant each time. Again if there are less than five judges it may be possible for a judge to make oversight of two incidents. At the other extreme if there is a very large number of

Patrols taking part then it may be possible for Patrols to move round the course in pairs. In these circumstances equipment provided and any specially required feature must be such as will enable two Patrols to carry out each incident simultaneously. Synchronisation of watches is necessary for simultaneous moving round and it is a good thing if one leader is free to make sure that Patrols are going to the right places.

Marking must be carefully done with each judge giving a mark, suitably out of ten, to each Patrol. Marks should be given for each stage in an incident. For example if an incident involves boiling some water and knocking over the dixie with an arrow fired from a bow, then, if need be, firing can commence without the water boiling but with appropriate loss of points on the boiling water part of the incident.

To a large extent the success of an incident journey depends on the intriguingness of the events. It may often be possible to use particular natural features in the vicinity of the campsite such as trees, a stream, a marsh, a wood or a dense area of bracken. Care must be taken that equipment and any natural feature is appropriate for what is being asked to be done. For example if a Patrol has to get itself and some stores into a tree to escape floods then the success of the incident will to a large extent depend on choosing a tree of just the right difficulty to climb.

The equipment which may be used for any incident must be carefully defined. It is not satisfactory if a Patrol carries round the course extra equipment for use other than perhaps personal knives. It may also be desirable to define that equipment supplied must not be damaged.

A judge must order any proceeding at an incident to cease or be modified if he considers it involves excessive danger.

The objective for each incident is carefully printed on a card and given to the Patrol Leader. It should be stated at the beginning of the event that the Patrol Leader must read out the card so that everyone knows what is going on. The wording of the card can be very important. There must be no ambiguities or means by which a Patrol can short cut an intended procedure. It may be necessary to give a few sentences of verbal explanation indicating for example which tree is to be climbed, the equipment which may be used or the boundaries of a supposed marsh. As a practical point judges must take care that Patrols do not carry on from an incident taking the card with them.

Given below are a number of incidents which have been found to work particularly well. There should be variety of incidents in any journey. Other incidents will no doubt suggest themselves to leaders especially using features in the vicinity of a campsite. Each incident is given a title and this is followed by the wording on the card. Notes are then given on equipment required and any other aspects to which particular attention should be given. In some cases suggestions are given on how the incident can be successfully completed in case it may be thought desirable to give hints with appropriate points penalty.

Floods

The river has burst its banks and the floods are rapidly approaching. You must get all your Patrol and all equipment, stores and water supply into the tree to a height at least 7 ft. from the ground before the floods arrive in ten minutes time.

The height from the ground can be variable depending upon the form of growth of the tree which must be neither too difficult nor too easy to climb. Lengths of rope and a couple of staves should be available to help possibly in climbing the tree and securing materials in the tree. Stores might consist of a large box, a sack containing material weighing about 30 lbs. and a large dixie filled almost to the top with water. A spare water supply must be available to re-fill the dixie if necessary.

Rare Orchid

Professor Beaufleur and his party are searching in Zaire for a specimen of the extremely rare orchid, *papyrus ruber*. The orchid lies on a magnetic bearing of degrees from the point indicated at a distance of not more than 50 yards. Find the orchid and pack it carefully for transit to Brussels.

A small artificial plant with a flower containing some red paper is constructed and hidden in reasonably rough ground not more than 50 yards from a given point. The bearing of the plant from the point is noted and written on the card. Equipment is a silva type compass, three Scout staves and a mallet. Success is usually achieved by ability to concentrate the search on the correct bearing. Staves are put into the ground to mark the bearing line up to a maximum of 50 yards and Scouts detailed to search along sections of the line. If the bearing read is not sufficiently accurate then correction by the judge may be given with loss of points. If finally necessary guidance should be given to find the orchid so that some points can be given for packing. One would expect to continue to use the same bearing and hiding point.

Obstreperous Horse

You are concerned that a rather obstreperous horse will come through a gap in the hedge and disturb your camp. Effectively block the gap with the material available so that you can pass the night with an easy mind.

The gap in the hedge can conveniently be represented by two trees growing about 6 ft. apart, by a genuine gap in a fence or hedge or by an open gateway or if need be by two Scout staves or other timbers driven firmly into the ground. Suitable material might be eight Scout staves and ten 8 ft. lashings. Other spars or branches can be made available. The important thing is that each Patrol has the use of exactly the same material.

Fallen Climber

You come upon a rock climber who has fallen from a cliff on to the beach and sustained severe internal injuries for which the treatment is absolute gentle handling and quick removal to hospital. The tide is coming in rapidly and you have no more than 12 minutes to move the patient to safe high ground 30 yards away to await the arrival of the ambulance.

The intention is that the Patrol constructs a stretcher using staves and lashings and move the patient with as much gentleness as possible within the time available. Equipment might be four Scout staves, which will allow ends as well as sides to the stretcher, and eight lashings for square lashings at the corners and a good lattice work base. There is of course no need for a cliff and the piece of safe high ground merely needs to be indicated. The smallest Scout in each Patrol can act as the fallen climber.

Electric Fence

In making an escape from a prison camp you are confronted by an electrified fence on which the slightest touch will result in electrocution. Every member of the Patrol must safely cross the fence using only the equipment supplied and no trace of the escape must be left. The fence is too high to clear with a running jump or vault and the party is too weak to climb up one upon another.

The fence which should be about 4 ft. 3 ins. high can be simply constructed by running lengths of twine about 1 ft. apart between two staves knocked into the ground about 12 ft. apart. The purpose of the reference to the party being weak is to prevent people climbing up on each other to leap over which the Scouts may try to do and which can be a hazardous operation. Suitable equipment is eight Scout staves and 11 lashings. An effective method is to construct a standard trestle with minimum 5 ft. long sides. The Patrol holds the trestle upright while one reasonably large and athletic Scout steadied by others climbs up and jumps over from the transom. Two staves are lashed at their ends to the transom about 15 ins. apart. The trestle is placed upright and the Scout already over the fence holds the free ends of the staves attached to the transom on his shoulders. Scouts successively climb up the trestle and crawl along the two staves. At the end the trestle can be lifted over by means of the two staves. Points are deducted whenever equipment touches the wire. The final measure of success is the number of Scouts got over without touching the wire.

Bow and Arrow

Light a fire, boil half a pint of water and knock over the boiling water with an arrow fired from a bow at a distance of at least 10 ft.

Equipment required is a small dixie, a length of twine, say 12 matches in a box and a small amount of paper if there is likely to be difficulty in lighting a fire for which there should be a piece of bare ground. There must be a reasonable supply of thin firewood. It is a useful additional factor if a Scout has to be despatched 200 yards or so to fetch water. If time is running out then attempts should be allowed to knock over the water even if it is not boiling. Apart from retrieving the arrow Scouts must remain behind the bow until the water is knocked over or time runs out.

Procession

The procession will be passing this spot in ten minutes time. Grandpa is very keen to see his old regiment go by but unfortunately he cannot see over the heads of the crowd. Construct a seat on which Grandpa can be raised so that he can view the procession in safety and comfort with his head at least 8 ft. from the ground.

A suitable tree is selected for this incident having a strong branch over which a rope can be thrown to pull up an improvised seat with someone sitting on it. In addition to an adequate length of strong rope there should be provided six Scout staves and eight lashings. The youngest Scout in the Patrol can act as Grandpa.

Arresting Enemy Agents

There are four enemy agents hiding in this wood. Your Patrol is to find and arrest them which can be done by touching any part of their person.

The need for this incident is a wood containing a large amount of fairly dense cover. An area of about 100 yards square will generally be suitable. It may be possible to define a restricted area of a larger wood.

Four small Scouts are required for this incident who are not taking part as members of Patrols in the journey, to act as the enemy agents. It will probably be best if they hide in the same places each time. None may be more than 6 ft. from the ground. Success is likely to depend on systematic combing of the wood. Points are given for the number of enemy agents caught. An alternative is to use the Patrol ahead in the incident course as the enemy agents. In this way the incident station can be used for two incidents. See next incident entitled Avoiding Arrest.

Avoiding Arrest

You are operating behind enemy lines and are in danger of being arrested by searching troops. If you can avoid being caught for the next 12 minutes you will be safe as your own forces will then arrive.

This incident is linked with the previous one entitled Arresting Enemy Agents using the same wooded area. Members of the Patrol hide where they want to in the area but not more than 6 ft. from the ground. Points are gained by avoiding being touched for the 12 minute period by the searching troops which consist of the Patrol behind in the circuit.

Snake Infested Ground

You find yourselves on ground where snakes of a particularly venomous species always emerge at 12 noon for a few minutes. The snakes can bite fatally but only to a height of 18 ins. You have 12 minutes to make a construction which will support all members of your Patrol at a safe height from the ground.

The basic equipment for this incident is three strong pioneering spars about 9 ft. long, three Scout staves or pioneering spars about 5 ft. long and eight lashings. A successful method is to make a tripod with the three long spars using a figure-of-eight lashing and then to lash the shorter lengths between the legs more than 18 ins. from the ground for the Patrol members to stand on.

Hidden Treasure

The treasure is to be found on the bearings written on the cards from the points indicated. Find the treasure.

The treasure can consist of a small tin containing a few sweets. Depending on the nature of the ground it can be hidden in dense undergrowth, long grass or bracken, or lightly buried in a bare earth or sand area or in a shorter grass area buried by carefully turning back turf. Bearings of the treasure are carefully taken from three clearly marked points and written on cards. Although only two points are in theory necessary a third is useful for confirmation. At least two compasses should be available and also four staves and two mallets.

It is important for this incident that it be in a position where finding or replacing the treasure will not be seen by Patrols still to come to the incident station.

Heavy Water Vehicle

A new vehicle powered by a heavy water fuel has reached the final test stage. The vehicle is kept hidden in the wood but is brought out for testing whenever it is thought it will not be detected by enemy aircraft. You are to bring out the vehicle along its runway (or take it back) within 12 minutes at the same time making sure that none of the extremely expensive and dangerous fuel is spilled. On no account may the fuel tank be touched.

The vehicle consists of a triangular pyramid. This can conveniently be made with six Scout staves with figure-of-eight lashings at the four corners though there should be a projection of one stave for about 9 ins. at each corner of the base forming lifting handles. The fuel is contained in about a 5 pint dixie which is filled with water to within half an inch of the top and suspended by twine from the top corner of the vehicle. The runway consists of a length of twine running from the hiding place in the wood out into open ground and passing through the vehicle. The twine does not run directly but may go slackly round a tree, through dense undergrowth, over a low branch and perhaps over a fence. The runway as defined by the twine can be about 40 yards long but can be variable according to the difficulty of the route chosen. The success of the incident is largely dependent on selecting a route which is neither too easy nor too difficult. Provided it is equally difficult to traverse the route in both directions then visiting Patrols may alternately bring the vehicle out and take it back. Points are given for progress made along the runway and for lack of spilling of water. Spare water supply is required.

INDEX

INDEX

Coding:

A = Active	N = Non-Active	L = Learning
I = Intensive Patrol	R = Reacreational	C = Competition
P = Part of Troop	T = Circuit (travel)	M = Special Material
E = Long (extended)	S = Short	K = Cooking
Y = Relay Formation	O = Outdoors	V = Variation

A full exposition on the method of coding and assembly into summary tables is given in Chaper III.